What people are sayin

The Journey into Oneself

Gopalakrishnan does a great job of exploring esoteric mysticism in his book *The Journey into Oneself*. What I really like about the book is that it is informative, yet a delight to read and a pleasure to absorb the ideas to becoming a better YOU.
Jody Long, Webmaster of Paranormal Phenomena Research Foundations nderf.org, oberf.org, and adcrf.org; attorney in Washington, New Mexico, and Louisiana

When you are on an inward journey to discover your Deeper Self, it is a very serious undertaking. But author Gopalakrishnan TC makes it possible for us to experience it as an adventure that not only informs and elevates but also brings us joy and cheer. He helps the reader navigate what he calls the Esoteric Field. Consequently, our meandering flow of life, with all its twists and turns, takes on new meaning and purpose. *The Journey into Oneself* is a book that can move the reader towards the goal of knowing the Deeper Self. It is made possible via self-transformation as you continue your inward journey by being a witness to yourself.
Narayani Ganesh, former Associate Editor of *The Times of India* and former Editor of *The Speaking Tree*

My son, who studies at Sholai School, brought your book to our house. Soon after, I wanted to put it in the shelf at the place where it belonged—as normally I am not used to reading this type of literature. One day, walking to the shelf I opened your book rather at the end, just to have a glimpse—and I got stuck, the words and their meaning straightly going somewhere deep inside. Now I am reading it from the end towards the beginning and I am deeply touched. It struck me as I could understand each and every word so easily and clearly because it is written so lightheartedly. I am so happy and grateful as I can feel I am not alone; I am part of an invisible community with similar experiences, with similar quests, with similar outlooks. I never had that understanding before.

I just want to thank you personally, congratulate you for your work and … also simply give you the joy of being approved.

Susanne KV, an appreciative reader, Kerala, India

The Journey into Oneself

An Exploration of Universal Spirituality

The Journey into Oneself

An Exploration of Universal Spirituality

Gopalakrishnan TC, PhD

MANTRA
BOOKS

London, UK
Washington, DC, USA

CollectiveInk

First published by Mantra Books, 2024
Mantra Books is an imprint of Collective Ink Ltd.,
Unit 11, Shepperton House, 89 Shepperton Road, London, N1 3DF
office@collectiveinkbooks.com
www.collectiveinkbooks.com
www.mantra-books.net

For distributor details and how to order please visit the 'Ordering' section on our website.

Text copyright: Gopalakrishnan TC 2023

ISBN: 978 1 80341 626 7
978 1 80341 665 6 (ebook)
Library of Congress Control Number: 2023945500

Design: Lapiz Digital Services

UK: Printed and bound by CPI Group (UK) Ltd, Croydon, CR0 4YY
Printed in North America by CPI GPS partners

We operate a distinctive and ethical publishing philosophy in all areas of our business, from our global network of authors to production and worldwide distribution.

Contents

Also by This Author

In Quest of the Deeper Self

978-1-43270-917-4

Dedicated to all those spirited people to whom the journey of life is an enigmatic adventure, coming up as it may with a pitfall or a fit pal!

Foreword

"When all the knots that fetter the heart are cut asunder, then a mortal becomes immortal. Thus far is the teaching."

"The self-existent Lord pierced the openings (of the senses) outward; therefore, one looks outward and not within oneself. Some wise people, however, desiring immortality, turned the gaze inward, and saw the indwelling Self."

Verses from the *Katopanishad*

"Life is a total process, the inner as well as the outer; the outer definitely affects the inner, but the inner invariably overcomes the outer."

J. Krishnamurti

The central theme of this felicitously written book is about the journey into the inner dimension of ourselves that the Upanishad and Krishnamurti refer to. The obstacles, "the knots that fetter the heart" we encounter in the course of this journey, are also observed.

On the global level, during the last four centuries the outward-going mind has operated with tremendous Vigor and given us the marvels of science and technology: Jet travel, computers, the Internet, painless laser robotic surgery and great cures for previously incurable diseases. Equally important is the fact that it has enabled the supply of running water and electricity to millions of homes. At the same time, modern science and technology have also created all the gruesome engines of warfare that killed or displaced more than 100 million people in the twentieth century, produced nuclear warheads and the atomic bombs dropped on Hiroshima and Nagasaki. Our world seems to be set on the 'balance of fear,' the nations being armed to the teeth with nuclear weapons.

On top of all this is the looming problem of the destruction of our living environment by our modern way of living, with the earth, air and waters of the world polluted beyond redemption. Our way of life in this Industrial Age has wrought destruction to all that sustains life on the Earth, threatening our very existence as a species on this planet. The outgoing mind has thus given us a double-edged weapon of great power that cuts both ways.

At the level of the individual during the early years, our outgoing minds are preoccupied with acquiring knowledge, earning a means of livelihood, raising a family and getting established in society. We spend long years well into middle age preoccupied with these outer concerns. But we are oblivious of and neglect to pay attention to what goes on in our own inner realm, in our hearts. This dimension is full of contradictory and conflicting impulses, suppressed desires and frustrations, hopes, fears, anger, self-pity, guilt feelings and so on. With his book *The Journey into Oneself*, the author Gopalakrishnan takes us on a journey into that unknown territory using as our guides the great contemporary spiritual teachers such as Ramana Maharishi, J. Krishnamurti, Nisargadatta Maharaj, to name a few, as also the past founding Masters such as Krishna, the Buddha and the Christ.

Coincidentally and felicitously, the author has chosen the Upanishadic metaphor of the 'knots of the heart' (he calls them the mental knots) to describe all the contradictory impulses in us that manifest as irrational behavior, outbursts of anger or as depression, causing so much unhappiness to ourselves and others. As the author points out, these unresolved and suppressed inner conflicts are at the root of all our outer conflicts in families, within a society, between nations and between religious groups; the daily newspaper headlines stand as testimony to that unfortunate scenario.

This book is an eloquent expression of the author's intention to help others to undertake the Inward Journey in a spirit of unprejudiced open-minded enquiry so that "the knots that fetter the heart are cut asunder" and we are enabled to lead happy lives, continuously exploring the unknown inner territory. Many spiritual teachers are quoted in the book, but the author speaks from personal experience and not from book-learning. That enhances the feel of its authenticity.

The Journey into Oneself is a book that reminds us of the fact that we neglect the inner dimension at our peril. It is well to remember Krishnamurti's saying, "The inner invariably overcomes the outer." This again is a reminder that unless we resolve our inner conflicts, the 'civil war in our inner space' we cannot resolve our outer, familial, nationalistic, religious and environmental conflicts.

O. Ramachandra Rao
Officer, Indian Administrative Service (Retired)
Trustee, Krishnamurti Foundation India, Chennai

Acknowledgments

Cosmic energy and intelligence are behind all actions in the Universe. Our level of awareness decides to what extent we are open to them. The more open we are the healthier is the outcome. So, we acknowledge their working through us and cooperate with them. The Divine flow helps us keep matters in order.

Coming down to Earth, many people played a major or minor role in helping the writer produce the book, after a production period that seemed to stretch like an elastic band. Before the band could snap, out came the book! Oftentimes, even a casual remark by some of them had a significant input. Grateful thanks are due to all of them.

The writer's parents, brothers and sisters have always given affectionate support to him from his young days, even as he tended to move into some unconventional avenues of exploration. Their confidence in him served to soften the rather stony grounds in that zone. In the recent past, his relatives and friends encouraged him in his attempt to bring out a book on the outcome of his reflections.

His brother Vasudevan and sister Vanajakshi showed keen interest in the book's progress. They also perused the manuscript carefully and raised some crucial points. Their appreciative remarks on some sections of the book served as a shot in the arm. The writer's wife Banumathy played an active role in following up with the book's development, reading the manuscript and bringing up some issues for careful attention. Her sustained support deserves appreciation. Banu's elder brother Seshadri presented the writer with a nice pen as soon as he heard that a book was being written. Her younger brother Suresh took pains to read the manuscript with the care of a mathematician and came up with useful suggestions. The writer's daughter Shuba is one of those who read the book in its early stages. She gave him an appreciative nod that kept his enthusiasm alive. His son Shankar went through the manuscript with clinical care. Listening to him convey the results of his systematic review was a matter of joy. Early on, niece Asha Sekar went through the first two chapters, felt tickled by an attempted joke there and laughed. It gave one the feeling that the book will fulfill its purpose!

Some friends played a significant role. Pramod Menon, Head of the English Department, Kodaikanal International School (KIS), India, studied the draft with the spirit of a friend and a reviewer. His comments and encouragement are appreciated. He looked askance at the originally intended title and so it underwent a change. Richard Mather-Pike, Web Designer, KIS, helped with the graphics. Prema Krishnan went through the manuscript with gusto. Her input infused the writer with confidence in general and, especially, on the lighter-vein aspects of the presentation. Lakshmi Venkataraman kindly agreed to give the book an editorial review. Her constructive criticism served to wash out some errors that played hide and seek in the text. Years ago, S. Sridharan brought the attention of the writer to two publications among others: *Siddhartha* authored by Hermann Hesse and *What Vedanta Means to Me* edited by John Yale. The profundity of the contents in them served as significant sources of inspiration to the writer. Excerpts from their pages are included in the present book.

The following publishers gave permission to quote lines from their publications. Their prompt and favorable response is gratefully acknowledged:

1. Yogi Impressions Books Pvt. Ltd., Mumbai
2. Ramanasramam, Tiruvannamalai, India
3. The Vedanta Press, Vedanta Society of Southern California, Hollywood

4. Chetana Pvt Ltd, Mumbai
5. Krishnamurti Foundation of America, Ojai, California
6. The International Association for Near-Death Studies, East Windsor Hill, CT, USA
7. Prof. Peter Singer, Princeton University, New Jersey, was approached in connection with permission to include an excerpt from his book *Animal Liberation*. Many thanks are due to him for giving the permission and for his kind and encouraging reply.

Chapter 1

Introduction

We are all co-passengers on this venerable journey of life. When we recognize this, there is a sense of togetherness and the associated camaraderie. If we add a note of empathy and celebration to this togetherness, the journey becomes vibrant and loveable. This book tries to delve into various aspects of the journey in order to appreciate our position as a traveler in this Universe and, consequently, bring about a brimming quality to our lives. Joyfulness becomes a significant accompaniment. It will inevitably spill over to our fellow passengers and add luster to their lives too.

It is said that the legendary swan of ancient India had a certain capacity: If we kept a mixture of milk and water in a vessel, the swan could just suck in the milk and leave the water behind. The same approach is suggested in reading this book, because the reader may find some items inspiring, some tolerably acceptable, some debatable and some totally unpalatable! It depends on the reader. So, take in what to you is milk and leave the rest to run down the drain. The idea of the book is not to impose any conclusion on the enthusiast but to expose the person to some relatively hidden regions of life for incisive reflections. The reader is encouraged to be an explorer treating the contents of this book as pointers. An investigative approach can always enrich one's life to the point of being able to love life's journey and make that love contagious.

Though some parts of this book do indulge in giving marginal directives, much of the matter is intended to be pointers whose value you put to test in the dynamic movement of life. Whether you are a believer or a nonbeliever, you are perfectly welcome; no precondition is stipulated. This book is intended to be a wayside companion. One is encouraged to explore the suggestions given and dig into the intriguing depths of one's being. The possible unfamiliarity of contents in some parts of the book may slow down the reading; that is where patient reflections are necessary. Such reflections can help one discover hidden truths and allow them to embellish one's life.

The spirit of the book is to act as a catalyst in bringing about growing self-awareness and cheerfulness in one's life through attention to certain issues that are usually overlooked. Such attention causes deeper understanding of life's journey and, hence, engenders a peaceful mind. That helps us face life's challenges in a constructive way and sustain our serenity. We may even go so far as to love life's vicissitudes.

In this book, readers will find themselves riding a cascade of serious expositions mixed with frivolous interludes. As always, a harmonious blending of the two can make our life healthy and happy. Thus, this book is expected to be not only physically light but psychologically too!

A huge ship amidst the oceans can only be turned slowly; its turn is imperceptible. When one pays attention to the journey of life for its own sake, life begins to turn imperceptibly towards vibrant waters. This ushers in a progressively calmer mind. There are no questions like, "Of what use is this journey to me?" Self-importance begins to wane out.

To highlight some points, excerpts are given at some places from the statements of Ramana Maharishi, Krishna, Jesus, Buddha, Lao Tzu, Adi Sankara, Nisargadatta Maharaj, J. Krishnamurti, Eckhart Tolle, and other Masters. The idea is not to impose authority but to give a punch to the pointers. Their words are pithy and deserve careful attention. Philosophic writers who don't belong to any system, such as Henry David Thoreau, and modern authors like PMH Atwater (on near death experiences) and Neale Donald Walsch (on dialogue with a Divine Voice) are also quoted at some places.

Appendices are given at the end of the book to highlight a few essential issues such as Advaita, the Monistic state of mind. If you wish to finish reading them before going on to the next chapter, it is quite alright. That will not put the cart before the horse; in fact, it may lubricate the cart's wheels!

Can one live one's life with abandon but, at the same time, not recklessly? Can one be serious about life's journey and yet be an affectionate bystander to it? It would be good to apply ourselves to discover the non-verbal answers to those questions. If this book had functioned as an aid in that direction, it would have fulfilled its purpose. Now, read on. Happy journey!

Chapter 2

Opening the Gates

There is a river meandering through the countryside, wide and sweeping in its flow. After the recent rains, it is brimming and flowing with some gusto. Schools of fish are having fun. An occasional boat with a rambunctious group streaks past and their laughter reverberates through the forest, gradually fading into the silence amidst the trees. You are aware of all this, and the growing aloneness gives it a touch of purity. Dancing waters of the river keep you company along with the rocks and the sand.

The sun is setting, and darkness is gathering amidst the trees. Suddenly, you are aware that this day and night are only local facts. Out there, in the vast space between the Earth and the Andromeda galaxy, there is neither the day nor the night; nor is there the day of the week. You return home, to the noisy turbulence of earthly life, and wonder about this great cosmic journey we are on. While religions do offer some solace and throw some light on the journey, they are limited because their zone soon becomes a playground of the ego. Such an approach is too narrow to appreciate the vastness of the journey of life. It is not suggested that we drop our religions but that we pay attention to *something* beyond the narrow-minded sectarian practices, beliefs and disbelief. That *something* can help us better appreciate the grandiose journey of life. It may be called the Esoteric Field. Herein lies an unlimited treasure. It goes abegging because people allow themselves to function within a very limited cocoon, controlled by the machinations of the ego.

This book deals with the Esoteric Field at length. Such a field is characterized by expanding awareness. Several pointers in the book aim at supporting the reader in one's enthusiasm towards exploring the Field. One may ask at this point, "What on earth is this Esoteric Field?" Patience! It becomes progressively clearer as you read along. Its essence cannot be captured through a mere verbal definition.

Cosmic silence and the timeless oneness of Divinity are behind all manifestations, like a movie screen that exists before, during and after the show. That is the metaphor often used by Ramana Maharishi. The screen remains untouched by whatever light and shadow move on it. As the cosmic process breathes in and out, the Divine drama goes on and life's journey moves on. This deeper awareness brings in a certain mental calmness and makes us treat the journey with deep respect. We no longer talk about "my life." Emphasis on 'I,' 'me' and the 'mine' becomes progressively weaker. That does not mean one becomes a pushover! There is a healthy outlook that brings in good-natured protest where necessary, while avoiding ego-manifestations. The resulting confidence moves one towards peaceful harmony. We see each one of us as a psychophysical system through which the venerable life flows on. Expanding awareness inevitably engenders deepening empathy and compassion. Under those conditions, one would never harm any living being. It leads to a spirited and spiritual life in which there is comprehensive care and, certainly, no room for fanaticism and violence.

The Esoteric Field, sometimes referred to in this book simply as the Field, is not something reserved for the few but is available for all who understand the impropriety of running along the conventional rut. It is like a parallel track to the routine one and it goes unnoticed because of the noise in our minds. This noise cannot be forcibly suppressed. Once we begin to sense the shallowness of life along the routine rut, we tend to move naturally into the Esoteric Field and the mental noise begins to subside of its own accord. Wondering about the Field, after some initial contact with it, causes the noise to go down further. The reduced mental noise makes us visit the Field more frequently, leading to further subsidence of the noise. It is this cyclic feedback that leads to our stable residence in the Field.

Being in the Esoteric Field does not mean that the person becomes an ascetic in the conventional sense of the word. It does mean an inward asceticism that does not in any way dilute a healthy practical life. In fact, it would help one apply oneself spiritedly to all aspects of life. Such comprehensive attention brings about wholesome living.

One can sense some wonderment as an essential undercurrent in the above process. This wonderment gently encourages us to pay attention to life's deeper values and understand the journey with an ever-widening perspective. Thus, each one discovers the Field in one's own way. There are no standard methods to put us in that serene zone. From the beginning there is a feeling of vibrancy because the whole thing flowers from within oneself. Life senses the receptivity of such a mind and exposes it to circumstances that take one towards deepening awareness. Help flows from many directions but no attachment to or dependence on any one source is entertained. There is, so to speak, an opening on all sides. Eagerness to learn increases and there is wholehearted acceptance of whatever life brings.

This book aims at bringing up several issues associated with self-awareness. As one reads along, quite a few issues spring up and provide the reader with areas for exploration. Thus, while reading, one may have to set aside the book sometimes and embark on reflections. Clarity resulting from those reflections can help one tide over difficulties in life with some equanimity. Simultaneously, we appreciate better the purpose of our presence on this planet. Like the light of dawn, inner clarity grows imperceptibly and steadily. It would become brighter and brighter and move us towards ever deepening harmony in the journey of life. You may find apparent contradictions between what is said in one part of the book and that which comes up in another part. With some persistence, you may find a hidden harmony between them and so the contradiction would disappear. They can function as paradoxes; going through them opens new windows. Further, some items may find repetition in various chapters. That means it is necessary to look at them in different contexts. Words alone cannot bring to light the deeper aspects of life, their ambience counts.

Most chapters in this book can stand by themselves though occasionally some cross-reference is made between chapters. A list of references is given at the end of the book; in the running text, such references are cited in the text with the author's name and the year. Liberty is taken to use capitals for the first letter of some words because of their prominence in the context of this book.

We are now on chapter 2. Next, chapter 3 describes a train journey in India. The train passes through variegated scenes. The purpose of the chapter is to emphasize the fact that relaxed attention to simple things occurring during the journey can take our attention into the hidden beauties of life. It would be a pity to use the travel merely as a means to an end. The vibrancy of the 'isness' of life is effectively brought out by the occurrences along the journey.

Some paradigms are introduced in chapter 4 as a forerunner to highlight a few essential issues that figure in the later chapters. It would be interesting for you to modify or extend them according to your own perception. After all, in some ways the journey is unique to everyone and, in the Esoteric Field, you are always out to strike new trails; that would be a departure from running along the well-trodden ones.

An important issue, Effervescence, is introduced in chapter 5. This is where the reader is mainly exposed to the characteristics of the Esoteric Field.

Chapter 6 deals with the common river as a metaphor for the dynamics of life. From time immemorial, the river has played an important role in the lives of human beings: As a source of fresh water, in the form of travel by boat, turning wheels to grind the corn, irrigating fields, providing scenic sites with their rapids and waterfalls, and so on. In this chapter, we look at some of the river's features that represent life's journey. The metaphor is highly relevant. It has particular reference to Prakriti, the Sanskrit word for the flow of nature with its own gamut of laws.

An important issue in human beings' lives is the thought-ridden noisy mind. This is also one of the chief items under the spotlight in the Esoteric Field. Its ramifications are reviewed in chapter 7.

The next chapter, chapter 8, is devoted to the transformation of the mind that takes place in an atmosphere of inwardly turned attention. The phrase 'Silent Mind' rings a bell in many people interested in understanding the deeper aspects of life, because we all somehow seem to know that proximity to Divinity is characterized by that inner silence. This is the content of chapter 8 where we dwell on the issue of clearing the mind of its centuries-old debris. Mental silence cannot be brought about through any effort on the part of the aspirant but only by sensing the beauty of passive awareness. J. Krishnamurti often refers to this as choiceless awareness. Eckhart Tolle's book titled *Stillness Speaks* (Tolle, 2003) has several pointers in that direction. While deep interest in the matter of mental silence is necessary for the change to take place, trying hard cannot help. The silent mind is one of a supremely relaxed state and, for it to manifest, struggling cannot be a forerunner.

A topic that most human beings would like to avoid is that of death. It is morbid. It is there at a distance; so, why talk about it now? They shroud it in fear and put it away. It is unfortunate that people should take such an unhealthy stand. The more one refuses to look at death, the more the fear grows. Further, when looked at with interest, the topic of death brings about a transformation in one's daily life and reveals such a fund of esoteric information that it would be a pity to hide from it. The conversation of Nachiketas with the Lord of Death in the Upanishads is indicative of the depth that death has as a topic. Here, chapter 9 deals with this subject. In recent days, a topic known as Near Death Experience (NDE) has caught the eye of many, especially of those who show interest in learning about what lies beyond conventional religious systems.

Chapter 10 is devoted to that which we all know to a good extent and to which we pay some attention: The physical body. A new concept is introduced around physical health; it is called 'The Second Line.' You can climb up to it, if you have not already done so, and even go beyond it, to 'The Third Line'!

Childlikeness has something to do with the transformation of the mind. As the mind evolves through the Field, it has the characteristics of a child's innocence sans the child's ignorance. What we all enjoyed as children begins to have value again but with a different philosophic implication of its contents. Self-importance is on the way out and abundant feelings flow towards everybody and everything. The spirit of adventure returns and one may again enjoy the stories of Tarzan and the Phantom! But each jungle picture now reveals a lot more than before and we may stop anywhere and linger on a particular item without rushing towards the end of the story just to see how Tarzan won! One may be ridiculed for being absorbed in kid stuff of that kind, but people are hardly aware that there can be as much message from it as from the scriptures! There is, of course, more to childlikeness than just getting a kick out of reading comics. Some attempts are made in chapter 11 to take a plunge into it.

Dos and Don'ts play a significant role in our lives. However, the Esoteric Field is not characterized by obedience to rules. It differs from conventional systems especially in this way and that is how it renders the mind free to explore. It does not mean that one is wayward in that region. On the other hand, a natural discipline sets in and so rules are not needed to keep one on the healthy tracks. The austerity that comes in without compulsion, and without conforming to rules, has great beauty about it. We dwell on this in chapter 12. However, to run the practical life smoothly, some suggestions in the form of Dos and Don'ts are given towards the end of that chapter.

There is a Japanese word: Satori. This is the state in which one's consciousness expands beyond the body and absorbs all things into itself. In the ancient Indian heritage, it is called the state of Advaita. It implies a merger with the Ultimate and a non-dual state of consciousness. The state of Enlightenment or Nirvana is characterized by it. A strange thing is that some ordinary beings, not necessarily sage-like, also fall into that state unexpectedly. They give us a spirited report about it but often find it difficult to describe it with the words of common parlance. Appendices 1 to 3 give narrations by those who went through this state. Satori does not come through any effort but only through a transformed state of the mind. It has nothing to do with piousness, hallucination or attachment to religious entities and scriptures. It is a ravishing experience, as reported by those who have gone through it; it has a touch of universality and of catharsis. Chapter 13 dwells on some aspects of Satori. The writer has not jumped into Satori yet but is acting here only as a microphone to those who know it firsthand. Sensing intuitively the profundity of that experience, even though it is someone else's, makes one acknowledge the intrinsic value of the experience.

Exposure to and reflection on the items brought up in this book can pave the way for some inner peace and the associated quiet mind. One can pick up the thread from there and proceed on one's own towards the seemingly unfathomable depths of oneself. The idea is to open the gates for an ever-increasing inward awareness that can help us appreciate our proximity to Divinity.

The last chapter, Epilogue, squares up the matter to end our journey through the book. Your actual journey of life, however, would continue. All the best!

Chapter 3

A Train Journey

In this chapter, we are going to enjoy a train journey by the *Vaigai Express* which runs between Madurai and Chennai in the southern part of India. It starts early in the morning and reaches Chennai around 2:30 pm. This journey has a few pointers that throw some light on our life's journey.

The early morning hours usually see freshness in our body and mind if we have had a good night's sleep. To start a train journey at that hour seems ideal. Our co-passengers are also equally fresh, and the atmosphere is salubrious in the air-conditioned coach. The porter who brings in your luggage arranges them in the overhead rack. You pay him more than what he asked for. He looks at you with eyes filled with gratitude and leaves. That lingering look on his eyes speaks from his heart and says more than words can. It remains forever etched in your mind. You settle down and watch others moving around a little, fidgeting for a while and getting settled. The train starts imperceptibly at the appointed hour, and for the next eight hours or so, the journey is going to put up many things for us to observe. Or ignore!

As the train leaves the big station, it has to meander across many tracks before it is free to travel on its own. In this process, it must go over sensitive steel points that get gently hit by the oncoming wheels. One can hear the metallic clang as this happens. After this zone is crossed, the engine wants to show its muscle in terms of its power and speed. On life's journey too there are such sensitive zones, and we must tread them with care. Thereafter, during the times we are on our own, like the train on its free track, it would be good to embark on reflection, contemplation and the like to deepen our self-awareness. Otherwise, our inner evolution slows down, and we may have to enter the next sensitive zone without the readiness to understand ourselves through the opportunities presented by that zone.

Now the train is picking up momentum. It has left the city and soon we are going through semi-wilderness. A look through the window shows vast areas untouched by man and the heavens in conversation with the Earth. Most passengers, however, are occupied with the newspaper or magazines. A religiously oriented person is chanting some mantras (holy verses) in a muffled voice. Some are lost in heavy conversation about a family or business problem. Then there are those strange characters that, soon after getting in, slump into their seats, doze off and get up just before their destinations! Perhaps, those passengers lost some sleep the previous night. It seems a pity to spend all the time on the journey in such oblivion. If one of them happens to occupy the aisle seat, we have a predicament! Keep watching to see if there is so much as a tremor in the person so you can excuse yourself on to the aisle, but the situation seems hopeless!

Then there are the people on their cell phones. Some talk in a low voice and keep the conversation short. There are others who finish a whole business deal on the phone itself, starting from signing the papers to sizing up the profits! Quite often these people are very loud, to the point of ignoring the co-passengers.

When at last the aisle passenger does show some movements and you get your chance, you move into the aisle. You haven't taken two steps on it; 'Smack,' something hits you on the knees from behind. You almost buckle on your knees but manage to straighten yourself and turn around to see who the perpetrator is. It is a three- or four-year-old that has been using the aisle as a playground and enjoying a Tarzan-in-action or some such thing. The child looks up and meets your eyes with an apologetic smile. What innocence in those eyes!

Immediately, all your irritation vanishes. Those eyes convey a great deal more than words can. Let us put this next to the porter's mute glance of gratitude. Those are occasions when the heart speaks, and the head remains silent. How often do we meet our relatives and friends with that language of the heart? Perhaps, people are inclined to say, "It is easy to do it to a stranger, but with regard to irritation from one's friends or relatives, it is a different matter." There is truth in this. Correspondingly, it can also be treated as an opportunity for exercising our awareness and helping both the offender and the offended to function from the deeper being. Here we listen to Eckhart Tolle (Tolle, 2003):

> How quick we are to form an opinion of a person, to come to a conclusion. It is satisfying to the egoic mind to label human beings, to give them a conceptual identity, to pronounce righteous judgment upon them.
>
> To let go of judgment does not mean that you don't see what they do. It means that you recognize their behavior as a form of conditioning, and you see it and accept it as that. You don't construct an identity out of it for that person.
>
> That liberates you as well as the other person from identification with conditioning, with form, with mind. The ego then no longer runs your relationships.

Back to the *Vaigai Express*.

Having recovered from the little one's onslaught, you move along the aisle, reach the doorway, open the door and, making sure you are safe, stand at the footboard. Oh, what a sight! The train is whizzing past a flat land, like a pan without a rim, with trees and shrubs all the way to the distant horizon. Occasional hillocks dot the skyline. It is a bright forenoon and the sun is throwing beams of light on the land through cracks in the cloud pattern. Here comes a rice field replete with water. It is the transplanting season. Some village women are planting the saplings, with their backs bent. As the train accosts them with its whistle, they straighten up to watch the carriages run past and, as it bids goodbye, their backs go bent again. Now comes a small but sparkling white temple with its clean precincts in the shade of a clump of trees; it is serenity personified!

Recent rains have made large pools of water on either side of the track and a flock of white birds (a kind of Jacana) is feeding in those pools. The speeding train whistles and the birds as a flock take to the air. The train hastily leaves the area and the birds come round in a large circle to settle back in their own spots to feed again. Here comes a level crossing. A bus, a car and a truck are waiting. There is a gentleman on a scooter. Sometimes you see a cow or a buffalo also waiting. They seem to know that after the train passes the gate will be opened. They have been with civilization long enough!

Here comes a small wayside station and the train is passing it at a good speed. The gusty winds from the speeding engine impinge on the row of trees over the platform. 'Woosh,' the broad leaves on the trees make a loud rustle as if to say a cheerful "Hello" to the train and its passengers. We whiz past the lonely stationmaster standing at the edge of the platform with a green flag stretched in front. Shall we spare a thought for him?

It is a particularly nice sight when the train is on a pronounced curve. We can see the engine majestically pulling its retinue of carriages at a good speed and whistling as if to say, "Come along, guys, we are winning!" This is a case where there is only the winner, no losers. We look toward the rear side and there is this long line of carriages following suit in humble obedience. Great sight!

Sometimes such a curve skirts around a mountain, and if you are standing at the footboard of the train, the mountain too seems to swing around with you. J. Krishnamurti's statement comes alive: "Those mountains are there with ageless vitality, timeless and immeasurable."

Sometimes you get a co-passenger who is neither too talkative nor too reticent. In the course of a casual conversation, you are exposed to a brief biography of that person. Anyone's biography has a touch of poignancy, a story spread over a thin sheet of melancholy with splashes of happy days here and there. Reflection on it helps us water down our judgmental tendencies and makes us be compassionate towards our co-passengers on the journey of life.

The noise of the wheels on the steel track has a rhythm of its own. Can we listen to it for some time, setting aside the problems and concerns that our thoughts want to feed on? The sound from the rolling wheels has a soothing quality and forms an unobtrusive backdrop to the train journey.

So many things go on during the journey, but most people are not interested. They will probably ask, "What is so special about these inane and routine happenings?" It is true that those occurrences have no market value. But those are the ones through which the Voice from Yonder speaks to us, a matter not to be confused with religious sentimentalism; however, it has the touch of the primordial religion uncorrupted by man. The 'isness' of life shines in our participation in those events and the heart begins to rule our lives rather than the head. Attention to such facts strengthens our awareness and we begin to see their effect in our relationships. It also seems to bring some order to our lives, both mentally and practically. In the absence of this, the 'me' gets hardened by repetitive self-cantered thought, the chief culprit in sustaining the ego.

Generally, the human tendency is to be hooked on to the result of a process rather than be in intimate association with the process itself. Under such circumstances, the present is passed by as unimportant. The process becomes merely a means to an end. It puts forth time as the future that is necessary for the 'I,' the ego, to continue. A purpose of this chapter is to alert ourselves to this tendency and to encourage us to be in affectionate contact with the process. In other words, can one be aware of things transpiring around one now, even though they appear valueless to the habitual mind? The train journey is a test.

It is not a healthy situation to keep the mind occupied all the time during the waking hours with some activity or the other. It is good to leave it free and see if it can remain alone without the dominance of thought. The train journey gives us an opportunity to exercise our attention in that direction. Then the same thing can express itself throughout our life.

Alright, here we are at the end of the journey. The train is majestically but gently buzzing into the terminus. The *Vaigai Express* has reached its destination. Its journey leaves an indelible impression in our minds. No matter how many times you travel by it, its grandeur remains undiminished.

Chapter 4

Some Paradigms for Reflection

An important aspect in our journey of life is the understanding of what may be called the esoteric side of our life. Some preliminaries of that aspect are explored in this chapter and we get into its full view in the next chapter.

Here the word paradigm is used in the sense of "a system of concepts and values that constitutes a way of viewing reality."

Human beings are subjected to a stressful life on this planet. Almost all of us get caught in the conventional streams of thought, and one's personal life gradually loses its glow. Even those who are socially successful realize, rather late in their lives, that they were chasing a shadow all along, a very deceptive shadow at that. Endless problems and difficulties leave many scratches in our minds and this attrition leads to a worn-out feeling. In order that we wake up to this early in our lives, we must turn to the Esoteric Field that leads us to a state of freedom essential for sensing the hidden beauties of life. It is this freedom that is capable of de-stressing our minds, steering us clear of the turbulent waters and moving us to peaceful ones. The outcome is irreversible; that is whatever peace and quietude that result from embarking on this esoteric journey stay and grow, never subside. Being alive to everyone and everything is the prime characteristic of the Esoteric Field. The past and future weaken their grip on the mind. Mundane issues will not lose their importance, but their values will be transformed, and they will shine in a more beautiful way. Also, the Esoteric Field forms the basis for understanding the more recondite issues, such as abiding in one's Deeper Self, even while carrying out one's mundane responsibilities in an efficient way. A movement in the Esoteric Field is meaningful only in terms of the journey itself and not in terms of any predetermined, expected end-result. It is its own reward. However, the journey is such that several healthy things happen spontaneously along the way, as by-products. An Indian sage of the past has said that all truly valuable things in the spiritual realm happen only as by-products.

We have to cover some preliminary grounds before we become familiar with the Esoteric Field as introduced in chapter 2. The truth is that we have all visited the Esoteric Field some time or the other in our life; we continue to do so, but we don't stay there long enough to appreciate its beauty and its ability to carry us towards the Ultimate. It is something like being drawn to a beautiful sunset while we are driving home. We may stop and enjoy the grand phenomenon. But we don't usually stay on it with a quiet mind long enough to let the impact permeate our consciousness. Not having enough time becomes the usual excuse. Further, there may be a tendency to compare it with other sunsets and make comments like, "The one I saw in San Diego last week was more beautiful." As a result, the noisy mind comes up and the contact with the beauty is lost. Something similar happens with regard to the Esoteric Field. In our childhood we enter the Field often, but as we grow in age the frequency diminishes and we tend to forget we were there at all!

So, in a way, all of us are familiar with the Field somewhere deep down in our consciousness. To bring it into our surface awareness, we have to pay attention to it in our daily life. In this book, we deal with some philosophic and psychological facts that pave the way to the understanding of the Field. With this in mind, we look into some paradigms to highlight those facts. Before we go into the paradigms, however, we must look into an important item related to our mental functioning.

Mentation

When our minds are confronted by problems in life, the usual tendency is to indulge in verbal analysis in order to get past the situation. Thought functions using the past knowledge to find a solution. In this process, what affects the analysis is the thought-created 'I.' Such a phenomenon is usually termed 'Mentation.' Even when there are no problems, the process is more or less the same. As this is repeated over many years, self-awareness gradually disappears from one's life. It is a kind of neurosis. However, as long as our outward behavior is within accepted norms, we are considered normal.

Some people come to sense the inherent impropriety behind this acceptable neurosis. This is because their lifestyle allows the deeper intelligence in them to wake up. Awareness sets in and the thought process itself comes under one's spotlight. Residence in the Esoteric Field is conducive to such awareness. Interest begins to focus on the mental breeding ground from where the 'I' emanates. This attention produces a healthy state and frees us from the above-mentioned neurosis. Gradually, one enters the deeper region within oneself, and the habit of mentation breaks down. One is no longer captured by thought as intensely as before; consequently, creation of the 'I' by the habitual thought becomes weak. Then our thinking runs under awareness. As J. Krishnamurti points out, the 'thinker' is seen to be a part and parcel of the thought process. It is a big relief; one's mind is unburdened to a considerable extent. A non-interfering witness attitude begins to prevail; it may also be called an affectionate bystander attitude.

Here it is interesting to note a well-known pointer from René Descartes, the French mathematician, scientist and philosopher. He was one of the first to oppose the Aristotelian approach because he could sense its limitations (Wikipedia). Descartes began by questioning knowledge based on authority, on the report of the senses and on mental reasoning. He found certainty in the intuition that, when he is thinking, he exists. This he expressed in his famous statement, "I think, therefore I am." It is a perception resulting from non-verbal reflection and self-awareness.

The Paradigms

In general, a paradigm brings together several interrelated items in a compact visual or verbal presentation using figures, symbols and words to elucidate a theme. It functions as a concise model and can be metaphorical in its approach. Items that relate to the human mind can be explained with simple paradigms. This chapter and the next present paradigms for the reader's reflection; they can help bring in self-awareness in daily life. There is nothing sacrosanct about the paradigms as presented here and it may be good to modify them to be more satisfactory models as per the reader's own intuition. Pondering over these models can take us to our inner realms. From there we can move on to a stable travel in the Esoteric Field.

Six paradigms are given here. They are captioned as:

The Two Circles
The Mental Knots
The Radial Dive
The Deep Ocean Peace
The Polarization and Convergence
The Inner Transformation

The Two Circles

Our daily mental state can be represented by two concentric circles and a zigzag line as shown in Fig. 1 below:

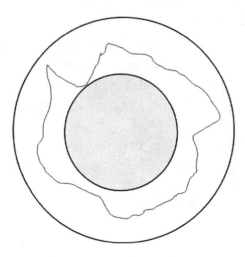

Fig. 1 Varying Mental States

The outer circle represents a very troubled state of the mind. In contrast, the inner one marks a calm and peaceful mind. In between the two is the zigzag line that indicates our actual mental state. During the day, it fluctuates and goes towards the outer circle due to the disturbance in the day-to-day affairs. After a good night's sleep, we are physically and mentally rejuvenated and so, usually, our minds come close to the inner circle in the mornings.

Stepping beyond the outer circle would mean that we have gone nuts! If that happens, people either commit suicide or go mad. Fortunately, this stepping beyond the outer circle does not happen easily and we are saved. Most of us, if not all, have enough emotional stability not to cross the outer circle. Stepping across the inner circle, into the green area, leads to a euphoric state. It is only occasionally sensed by grown-ups. Our aim of exploring the Esoteric Field is to let it help us glide into that sublime region. However, the primary thing is to understand what brings us close to the inner circle during the waking hours. It is part of an interesting expedition into oneself. That can bring in some joy and the associated nonchalance.

Each one must discover the factors that take one near the inner circle and those that push one away from it. This focuses our attention, as part of our self-awareness, on the mental and physical activities of our daily life. Being caught in incessant thought is one of the main reasons for going near the outer circle. Later, in chapter 7, we explore the noisy mind and discover the process of being trapped by thought during waking hours. Attention to this matter of two circles brings a certain order in our lives and progressively takes us closer and closer to the inner circle. Certain childlikeness begins to play a role in our daily life and childishness gradually disappears. It is interesting to watch the transformation as it takes place due to our diligent enquiry into what brings us close to the inner circle. Many down-to-earth items, such as diet, sleep, exercise and sports, also get examined in this process. However, the primary thing is the inward exploration through self-awareness that brings about the transformation conducive to moving closer to the inner circle, and then into it.

The Mental Knots

Here also we describe our mental state by two concentric circles. As seen in Fig. 2, some knots appear here and there between the two circles.

Each knot represents an energy pocket in our minds as a result of some attachment or resentment; for example, the attachment to a nation. During our interactions we usually react from these knots. We feed energy to these knots through thought; the intensity of reaction from a knot depends on how energized it is; that is, on how strong the attachment or resentment is to the matter represented by the knot. In short, these knots are the functional abodes of the ego. When thought feeds on them, the knots get wound like springs. The reaction from a knot is like a spring lashing out. The stronger the attachment, stronger is the reaction. In other words, the stronger the attachment the more 'knotty' we are!

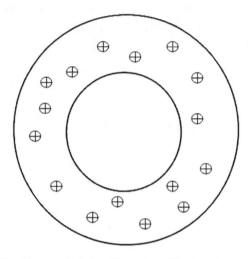

Fig. 2 The Knots and the Knot-free Region in our Minds

Our knotty behavior is not so much because we are naughty but because we are haughty! Apart from its incidental rhetoric, that sentence has an intrinsic truth about it. Each knot functions as a center for the ego and that is what makes our behavior ego-centric in general.

Attachment usually flows along three avenues, namely, attachment to people, to things and to ideas. Here 'things' include living beings like dogs and cats too. A person may be attached to the idea of communism or agnosticism or nationalism. Or, that person may be against them. Both the negative and positive attachments create knots. Thus, each one of us develops a number of attachments and our waking hours are usually spent functioning from those knots. It results in a strongly externalized mind, a mind primarily hooked on ego-based issues. It is the main reason for mediocrity in life. Generally, we remain unaware of this unhealthy situation.

An important question comes up now. While ego manifestations are unavoidable when acting from the knots, is there such a thing like acting from outside the knots? The answer is YES. When we act in pure compassion, it is from the knot-free region. Also, when we are concentrating on some item of practical work, the ego is temporarily absent, and we don't act from a knot. Let us now consider the following questions:

1. When we are not engaged with something, can we remain outside the knots? If we are not alert, the thought vortex pulls us into one of the knots and, unknowingly, we keep winding its spring. In chapter 7, we note the existence of eight such vortices.
2. Can the knots be allowed to dissolve leading to a deeply relaxed state of mind?

Reflection on the above questions makes us take an inner dive into ourselves. We begin to perceive what it means to function from outside the knots. Alert awareness keeps us from falling into a knot and we enjoy responding from the knot-free region. Once we taste this, we begin to relish the action and become increasingly interested in it. We notice that compassion rules in the region outside the knots. To that extent, life is tension free, and we would make others happy.

The awareness thus created through functioning from outside the knots grows stronger and begins to dissolve the knots. Also, we now become conscious of how a knot is created and so there is a chance to nip it in the bud. The process of how the spring of a knot gets wound is also clear. These are sensed non-verbally and that very sensing begins to act. Awareness of the spring being wound stops that action. This is what Adi Sankara called "Sakshi Chaitanyam," that is 'Witness Consciousness' (Sankaranarayanan, 1988). In other words, it is the non-interfering, affectionate but alert witness attitude that brings about the needed transformation.

Concern is also a form of attachment. The knots cannot be pushed out through effort because it would mean that we have now developed a new concern, about how to push out the knots! It is like creating a new knot. That leads to a dilemma: One cannot go on with the knots and one cannot make efforts to push them out either. The situation looks hopeless. Each one has to solve this intriguing puzzle for oneself because the answer has to come from deep inside and not from others or from one's thought-ridden mind. Again, the answer is non-verbal. Being aware of the knots in action, and the associated reflections, can take us to the inner realm, from where the answer springs up.

Strong attachment to a religion, nationality, race and the like creates powerful knots and unleashes violence, creating great harm to human beings. Even petty family and other quarrels emanate from this knot-syndrome. Hence, happiness in our personal and collective life depends on how knot-free we are or, at least, to what extent we don't function from the knots. In the Enlightened Beings, there is absolute freedom, and all the knots would have undergone dissolution.

The Radial Dive

Our minds are usually externalized; they get hooked on to things happening in the world, with special reference to 'I,' 'me' and the 'mine.' We develop corresponding images in our minds. At the social level, this is very much encouraged. Our minds then carry on with the noise created by the images and sustained by thought. Fear, anger, sadness, desire and self-pity occupy most of our waking hours. To some extent, people step out of these through intelligent application; however, most of the time thought dominates and we function from the knots, as in the previous paradigm. Seriously-minded people do apply themselves to discover ways to find peace and calmness in their lives. But, in this process, most of them adopt the analytical approach. This works along the circumference of a circle as shown below. The analytical approach is limited by the content of the mind, and hence it cannot produce a radical change.

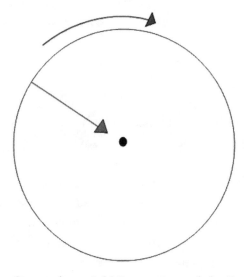

Fig. 3 The Circumferential Movement and the Radial Dive

There is another approach that may be called the Radial Dive. Here, even though logic is used, the understanding is due to non-verbal sensing. This is shown in Fig. 3 by the radial inward line in contrast to the circumferential movement. Perceptions developed in the ancient heritages, such as that of India and China, are examples of the Radial Dive. Philosophies produced by rational thinkers like Bertrand Russell, Alfred North Whitehead, Karl Marx, and similar analysts belong to the circumferential type. Rational philosophies can be remarkably interesting and stimulating to the intellect. They may also sometimes produce marginal changes in one's psychology. But they cannot bring about fundamental transformation in our minds. This is because transformation takes place due to Direct Awareness that does not rely merely on logic and verbal knowledge. In such a process, the rational mind becomes an obstruction, because it is like a part of the mind trying to analyze the whole. Direct awareness associated with the Radial Dive is based on intuitive sensing; it flows from the whole to the part and on to the whole again!

Enlightened Masters have always emphasized the value and beauty of the Radial Dive. A few centuries ago, Meister Eckhart and Marcus Aurelius spoke from perceptions originating from such a dive. In modern times, presentations from Alfred Aiken of the United States (Aiken, 1997) and Eckhart Tolle from Europe (Tolle, 2001) indicate the outcome of the Radial Dive.

As we can see from Fig. 3, no amount of circumferential movement can take us closer to the center, whereas even a small displacement along the radial dive does it. From ancient times, the Indian and Chinese cultures had understood the value of Direct Awareness for discovering the deeper and hidden aspects of life, body and mind. Intuition was treated superior to the intellect. This led to their discovering Monism as a perception superior to Monotheism. There were also some cultures of Europe, such as that of the Druids, which brought out the value of Direct Awareness. Currently, individuals who show capacity and interest in this radial movement form a small minority of the world's population. They are found all over the world and are not confined to any group. They enter the Esoteric Field and become an inspiration to the others who show keen interest in understanding life's journey.

When we listen to the talk of an Enlightened Being, we can feel Direct Awareness taking us over and our rational mind receding to a back bench. The same thing takes place when we read a book depicting their talks. As an experiment, to get an idea of Direct Awareness, one can try listening to one of their recordings. Our minds lose their compulsive hold on us and there is an inner thawing-out. The associated calmness can be described as a lingering feeling of non-action.

The Radial Dive proceeds from a quiet mind and ends in a quiet mind. An interesting exercise is to discover the Radial Dive in our daily life. It has the capacity to dislodge a lot of the burden from our minds as it is non-accumulative in its approach. The more we are at it, the more the elbow room in our minds, and this clearing brings about inner silence. It is a purging that has the capacity to clear centuries-old neurological debris inherited by us as a member of the human race. We thus flow into our deeper realms and come close to the inmost zone in Paradigm 1.

Knowledge acquired from religious scriptures and other books usually becomes intellectual baggage. It moves one along the circumferential path rather than along the radial line. Later on, in chapter 12, the difference between a religious preacher and an Enlightened Master is brought out in terms of their presentations. Here the following pointer from Nisargadatta Maharaj (Dunn, 1997) is worth noting:

> First of all, you abide in your own self and transcend it, and in transcending, you will realize the Ultimate. The words emanating here are not borrowed knowledge which is available in scriptures and other books; this is from direct experience. *Nirupana* means the normal practice of these professional spiritual people; they will be expounding knowledge from various books.

The Deep Ocean Peace

Our mental states can be likened to the ocean in some ways. Currents, tides and waves affect the ocean waters. Our minds are affected by analytical thoughts, emotions and feelings. Waves disturb the surface of the ocean only, not so much the deeper waters. Similarly, in our minds too, it is the surface layers that are shaken by disturbing circumstances. People may feel that some disturbances go very deep. Still, there are much greater depths of the mind that remain unaffected by any experience, no matter how disturbing it may be. This may sound strange. It is because, during the waking hours, we are aware only of an exceedingly small part of ourselves. Now, let us examine the following figure, Fig. 4.

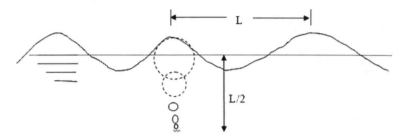

Fig. 4 Waves on Ocean Waters

The water waves are characterized by successive crests and troughs. Distance between two adjacent crests is known as the wavelength, denoted by 'L' in the figure. Progress of the wave takes place by the water particles performing circular orbits around their initial position. It is to be noted that water particles do not move along the wave. Only the disturbance moves as particles transfer their energy to successive ones after being initially excited by some force like the wind. If we drop a stone in a pond of still water, ripples travel away from the epicenter in ever-expanding circles. Now, if we drop a leaf at a distance from the epicenter, we notice that the leaf dances around an average position but does not go with the wave. This proves that water particles perform an up and down and horizontal motion around their original position. The radius of the vertical circular motion of surface particles can be termed as the amplitude of motion. The next fact is that water particles successively below the surface also get excited because of their proximity to the surface but, as we go down, the amplitude of disturbance gets progressively diminished.

The physics of water waves tells us that the amplitude becomes smaller and smaller until it is negligible at a depth of half the wavelength. Below that depth, the water particles don't know that there is a wave going on top. They couldn't care less! Peace reigns.

In the expansive oceans, waves of lengths up to 250 meters have been noticed. This means that wave disturbance reaches only 125 meters below the surface, this depth being half the wavelength. Compare this with the depth of water in the deep oceans ranging up to several thousands of meters. At the deepest part of the world oceans, the Mariana Trench in the Pacific Ocean, the depth is approximately 11 kilometers. So even when a storm is raging on the surface and creating giant waves, much of the ocean waters remains undisturbed. Our minds function much the same way. It would be good to explore through the inwardly turned awareness whether there is that stillness below the superficial layers of the mind. Phenomenal patience is required to take our center of attention to that zone. The advantage is that just embarking on this quest already begins to change our lives, giving one the feeling that something good is happening.

Eckhart Tolle (Tolle, 2003) gives us a pointer in this connection. He says that feeling the energy of our inner body, the mental activity slows down, and one is submerged in a deep sense of aliveness below the turbulent emotions on the surface. The 'aliveness' that Eckhart talks about is the very nature of self-awareness.

The deep ocean stillness is always with us but because we live on the surface during the waking hours, we become unaware of it. We all enter that deep ocean zone during the period of dreamless sleep. In our waking hours, if we can go below the surface and understand what it means to function from that mental peace, our lives will be transformed to one of serenity and equanimity.

The Polarization and Convergence

For this paradigm, we consider an iron piece before and after magnetization. As shown in Fig. 5 (a) below, the non-magnet has its internal elements thrown helter-skelter with regard to their north-south polarity. The result is that opposite poles cancel each other, and the net magnetic effect is zero. During magnetization, those elements are aligned by the magnetizing force such that their directions are polarized, as shown in Fig. 5 (b). Here the small internal magnetized elements cancel each other's effects but at the ends of the bar there is concentration of the same polarity. That is how the bar becomes a magnet with pronounced opposite poles at the ends.

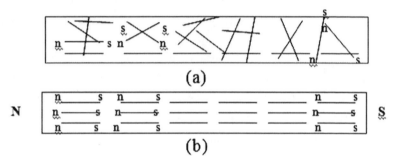

Fig. 5 Elements in the Non-magnet and in the Magnet

The analogy here is that our mental elements are also, in general, aligned helter-skelter. When polarized, they function in a synergistic way and make the mind respond with some orderliness. Wastage of mental energy is avoided. Here we note that attention to the Esoteric Field has the same effect on our minds as the magnetizing force has on the iron piece. Polarization takes place in our minds and, to that extent, we feel peaceful. Increasing mental orderliness ushers in confidence. Such unhealthy habits as smoking, drinking and the like drop out in the Esoteric Field because the polarized state is an inherently healthy state of mind. Addictions cannot enslave such a mind. One keeps off the negative things in life without any effort. Good things happen as by-products consequent to our residence in the Esoteric Field.

The un-polarized mind hits physical health too. Correspondingly, when it is polarized, bodily illness begins to disappear. This is one area where effects are seen fairly early in one's application to the inner dive.

Mental *polarization* is followed by *convergence* of the energies towards the Inner Being. This situation augments the Radial Dive and mental silence deepens. The state of the mind becomes conducive to discovering what lies beyond the apparent. Vibrancy resulting from the convergence adds a spiritual quality to our daily lives.

The Inner Transformation

We are all familiar with the thought-ridden mind. Our waking hours are entirely captured by the habitual thought. Most of us carry on with this, not sensing the great harm such mentation does to us by sustaining the ego. The noisy mind is responsible for all evil in both the individual and the collective. That is why even severe punishment by the law is unable to bring down crime in society. Without the law it may be worse, but with the law too it is bad enough. Then there is the war between tribes, countries or other groups, a sad scenario indeed.

People do get concerned about this and rely on religion and meditative methods to bring the unruly mind under control. This does produce beneficial effects and engenders certain orderliness in those adherents. However, deep inner transformation cannot be brought about by those methods. The reason is that the ego takes hold of those approaches and uses them to its own advantage. That is why there are quarrels and wars in the name of religion itself. Thus, no system or technique can be effective. Further, such things rely on the past to bring about a change in the future. In contrast, there can be a thing like action in the present which alone can produce a Radical Transformation. This action is related to self-awareness that is choiceless and motive free. Talks of Ramana Maharishi, Nisargadatta Maharaj, J. Krishnamurti and similar Masters are directed towards making us understand how self-awareness sets in. In the wake of this understanding, Radical Transformation takes place of its own accord. Those Masters do not prescribe any religious or meditative techniques. They do make suggestions that appear like methods but no technique can be carved out of those suggestions.

A word of caution is necessary here: If your gut feeling tells you to follow a method or technique, it would be good to go through it. Go along with it and see what happens. If it shows signs of freeing you from fear, regret, attachments and the like, well and good. If it only serves to produce ego satisfying results, then, obviously, this is counterproductive.

Fig. 6 depicts the gradual transformation in the state of mind as awareness deepens. Six zones are recognized. The demarcation between the zones is hazy. Each zone overlaps the adjacent ones to some extent. It is interesting to watch the center of consciousness move through the zones as awareness progressively clears the ground. The basis and contents of the zones are explained below.

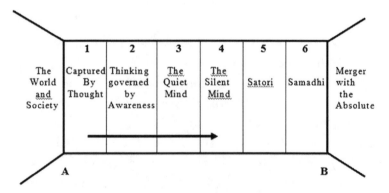

Fig. 6 Stages of Transformation in Growing Awareness

On the left extreme in Fig. 6, we have the world and society. The externalized mind is occupied with matters associated with them. From A to B are the changing features of the human mind as a result of inner transformation. In the first zone, named as 'Captured By Thought,' the mind is occupied by thoughts almost all through the waking hours. Part of this occupation is with purely practical matters when the ego is not operative. The rest of the times, the mind is controlled by thoughts driven by 'I,' 'me' and the 'mine.' This is the destructive part that causes harm to the individual and the collective. That represents the action from the knots mentioned earlier in this chapter. In this connection, some Masters point out that most of this activity is unnecessary, while much of it leads to painful consequences.

Due to the Radial Dive, awareness sets in and one sees the intrinsic harm in being caught by egoistic thoughts. It is this seeing that makes one move towards the second zone, namely 'Thinking governed by Awareness.' This does not take place all of a sudden but in fits and starts at the beginning. Interest in that direction brings about some steadiness in remaining in the second zone. It is an evolution. That is why it was mentioned that the line between them is hazy. Mental alertness in the individual releases the person from the tyranny of thought and firmly establishes the center of consciousness in the second zone.

In this zone energy wasted through thought becomes less and less. It slows down the physical aging process too, to some extent. One begins to understand the machinations of the ego and its destructive effects on mental peace. Such things like persecution complex cannot function in the second zone. Further, mental states like boredom and loneliness are on the way out. One begins to sense the value of a quiet mind without there being an imposed control over the mind. Pure awareness is seen to do the job.

As a result of the aliveness created by the second zone, the center of consciousness moves to the third zone, 'The Quiet Mind.' Here thought as habit does not function except for attention to practical matters. Our tendency to deal with people through the image we have about them is removed and an 'aliveness' comes into the interactions. Compassion rules our relationships. Since one's ego does not manifest, the other's ego does not get triggered either. Two people meeting under that condition are like two souls meeting, a very joyous and life-supportive experience. We note that the word soul here represents the Sanskrit word Athma; that is the Divine Spark in us without any identifications. The mind becomes intrinsically religious and not religious according to a system. That state of natural religion has no belief or disbelief associated with it and so is uncorrupted by man. It has the touch of universality, like all fundamental truths have. This universality implies that, in that region, there can be no such things as 'my religion—your religion,' 'my God—your God' and such ego-based shallowness.

Up to the end of the second zone, a certain depth of interest in the individual is needed to bring about the transformation. Beyond that zone, pervasive consciousness takes over and does the rest. Silence moves in cataclysmically as a result of the mental state provided by the quiet mind. It is like keeping the house clean for the Guest to arrive. Just as we remain open for the Guest to arrive, we must be passive until silence streams in. It may take its own time but there will be no anxiety because the ego no longer drives the mind. One takes one's hands off completely from the process; that leads to effortless detachment. It gives the mind the required state of relaxation to take in the silence. Our minds need some inherent robustness arising out of the ego-free state to receive the Divine Guest. The process is one of euphoria. There is a feeling of being completely swept by the phenomenon and its momentous entry. It is a catharsis. People may go through some body aches at that time but as the mind does not put up any resistance to the aches, there is no suffering. Soon the body settles down to a new rhythm, the aches are gone and all is well.

Then, the center of consciousness moves to the fifth zone 'Satori.' As mentioned before, this Japanese word connotes an expanding consciousness moving out of the body. Oneness with everything is experienced in this state. The book *Leaving the Body* by D. Scott Rogo gives us an idea of what happens when consciousness expands pervasively (Rogo, 1983). The following lines give the essence of a presentation excerpted from that book.

> People who undergo an out of body experience get a peak feeling that makes them blissfully merge with all creation. It has a profound impact on the way they view life. They tend to appreciate life better, show sincere respect for others, while adopting a more mature and healthier attitude in all aspects of their life.

If you read accounts of people who have had an out-of-body experience or a near death experience, you may feel a pull towards the beauty of inner transformation. It is a good feeling and it means that your center of consciousness has already moved deeply, as envisaged in this paradigm.

Appendices 1 and 2 depict narrations by two people who went through Satori. An important aspect of their narrations is their attempt to describe the tremendous silence and the timelessness while being bathed in it. The author of the article in Appendix 3 also describes some characteristics of Satori.

During the period Satori begins to settle down in a person, great changes take place both in the body and in the mind. When the process is complete, the person settles down to a new rhythm physically and mentally. This well-established state of freedom is known as Samadhi and is depicted by the last zone in Fig. 6. Here the individual identity is completely dissolved. A merger with the Ultimate has taken place. This is Enlightenment or Liberation. Death of the body becomes irrelevant to an Enlightened Being because consciousness has already released itself from the body. For the people around, however, such a person's demise feels like a big loss because guidance from an Enlightened Master is no longer available. Thereafter, the guidance may operate in some intangible form.

Whoever is attracted to this inner transformation will do well to cooperate with that Divine call and guide their daily lives in accordance with it. There is no better way to help oneself and humanity. Once the center of consciousness begins to take the inner dive, many good things happen as by-products. These are first felt by oneself, next by one's kith and kin and then by others. Primarily, compassion rules one's life and man-made divisions no longer influence one's outlook. The élan associated with the transformation is said to be magnificent.

Chapter 5

The Effervescence Euphoria

In chapters 2 and 4, the concept of Esoteric Field was introduced. We explore the characteristics of that Field in this chapter. This is initially done using what may be called an Effervescence Model. Dictionaries give the meaning of the verb Effervesce as:

1. To bubble, hiss and foam as gas escapes
2. To show liveliness and exhilaration

Both meanings are relevant with regard to the Esoteric Field. Transcending and rising above the conventional life pattern refers to the first, and the aliveness associated with the Field belongs to the second.

Fig. 7 below depicts the way people effervesce above the conventional mindset and begin to function on their own. This aloneness, as different from loneliness, is a characteristic of the Field.

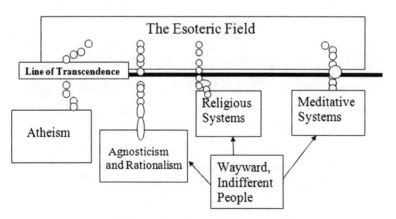

Fig. 7 Effervescence and Transcendence

The Transcendence

Fig. 7 shows how people go through different systems and how some of them effervesce into the Esoteric Field. All boxes are shown to be below the Line of Transcendence because they all have one thing in common: they force their adherents to conform to a set of beliefs and conclusions and thus to respond from a conditioned state of mind. Herd mentality becomes a necessary concomitant. Most people do not want to leave the box they are in because it provides them with two crucial factors: Ego satisfaction and ego security. These are derived from logical and emotional attachment to the system. The adage, "One believes what one wants to believe," is relevant here. As a result of sustained contact with the system for many years, the attachment gets hardened and it becomes exceedingly difficult to release oneself from the box.

The cleverly woven conceptual fabric of the systems has a stranglehold on its adherents. Nevertheless, some feel the need to outgrow the attachment because they sense the inherent impropriety of being a slave to a system. They begin their transcendence and move on to the Esoteric Field. This takes place when their native intelligence gets the better of them and makes them understand that the edifice they have carefully built in the name of their system turns imperceptibly into a prison. It is a rigid psychological confinement. Such confinement causes fear of meeting unfamiliar things and it blocks the mind's freedom to explore. This is the case with the general humanity today.

There are some people, however, who take the liberty to interact with other systems and reduce the rigidity of their confinement. People of that kind usually show tendencies to effervesce into the esoteric region. Transcendence may take place from any of the systems depending on the individual psychology. The wayward and indifferent people do not effervesce directly but go through some system before their inner evolution takes them to transcendence.

People in the lower levels of a system show greater attachment and fanaticism than those who grow into higher levels in the same system. At higher levels, they tend to spill out and pay some attention to the contents of the other systems. This learning process creates some elbow room and the confinement imposed by the box begins to melt down. Eventually, those people effervesce.

Whenever a thing is rightly transcended, there is neither residual attachment nor residual resentment towards that thing. There is only a feeling of affectionate detachment from it. That is the mark of true transcendence.

A person in the Esoteric Field feels like a citizen of the world, a member of humanity and not a member of a particular nation, race or religion. That way, one clears oneself from the influence of group psychology. It is to be noted that group psychology differs from mob psychology only in degree, not in kind. This sensing is what makes one release oneself from all man-made and man-influenced systems.

The Nature of the Esoteric Field

A salient feature of the Esoteric Field is that there are no systems to identify oneself with. People in this region do not hold hands and say, "We belong!" Aloneness is the very essence of the psychology there. Thus, the herd-mentality and group-fanaticism are clearly dissolved; one's freedom to explore is sustained. While they do help each other in feeling the deeper aspects of life's journey, groupism does not take place. It makes one flow freely into oneself and discover the meaning of "Know thyself." Such an inward movement of awareness carries one towards feeling the proximity of Divinity, beyond all religious and philosophic concepts. In the region below the line of transcendence in Fig. 7, beliefs and conclusions have a stranglehold on people; they begin to evaporate as one ascends to the Esoteric Field. Freedom from tyranny of conclusions paves the way to a quiet mind. With this inner quietude, there is the enhanced ability to perceive what lies beyond the apparent. The beauty of non-verbal perception becomes a salutary concomitant.

Even though a person in the Esoteric Field is freed from group psychology, attachments to newly found conclusions may remain in the individual and cause individual fanaticism. However, this takes place only in the initial stages of moving into the Field. Soon after, it begins to dissolve because of the eagerness to learn and the growing self-awareness. This atmosphere of humility is endemic to the region.

There are several issues that highlight the Field, looking at which the reader can appreciate that field's exalted nature. An important characteristic of the region is that one becomes charged with enthusiasm for sensing what lies beyond the apparent and for living vibrantly. The all-encompassing love that people feel as a result of a near death experience is sensed here as a growing feeling. Self-centered, utilitarian drives for personal salvation or aggrandizement begin to wane out. Movement in the Field is one of discovery rather than conformity to a system. That kind of search and discovery adds a strange quality to life; the ego begins to take a back bench and to progressively give way to expressions of the Inner Being. As the reader can guess, this thing does not take place by following a bunch of instructions as Dos and Don'ts. What is required is a spirit of adventure and the associated explorer's inquisitive outlook. There is freedom from attachment to the image of oneself foisted by society on one.

The essence of the Esoteric Field lies in the quality of deep passivity and in understanding the movement of life, its beauty and purity. It is not guided by self-satisfying notions of spiritual achievements and rewards. Humility helps one avoid arguments and quarrels.

The power of passivity and the associated intrinsic transformation cannot be of value to the thought-ridden mind.

While such transformation furthers itself and becomes all comprehensive, no correction in it will ever be needed. The movement of understanding due to non-interfering self-awareness does not allow such tricky factors as pious egoism to rule the roost. (Pious egoism is a state of contrived humility.)

Since there is no institutionalization in the Esoteric Field, each person there shines like a "Single Star in a Limpid Sky," an expression used by J. Krishnamurti in connection with aloneness. It needs certain courage to remain alone inwardly. That unshakable confidence comes from the following:

1. Non-dependence on a system or person to provide the base for security and satisfaction.
2. Understanding that life is a friend who is always helping us move towards the Ultimate.
3. The sensing that each one of us is given all the resources needed to return Home, to Divinity.
4. Feeling the Inner Being's inscrutable but unshakable support in daily life.

Factors as above bring a natural austerity to one's life and so there is an unforced discipline in the conduct of such a person. Kindness and respect for everyone govern that person's actions. As of now, those who have transcended to the Esoteric Field make up a small minority on this planet. That is why there is so much violence in the world today, inflicted not only on man but on other living beings as well.

Some living Masters tell us that our urgent task in the present stage of human evolution is to go beyond the thought-ridden state of mind, thus freeing us from the harm that such a mind does to the individual and the collective.

The Practical Side: Generally, people look for some kind of technique or method to reach a predetermined end. This is absolutely necessary in the practical field. However, in the matter of spiritual awareness, this becomes counterproductive. The reason for this can be explained as follows.

When a person wants to achieve something from which the 'I' will be benefited, the mind puts forth time in the form of psychological future; that is, "I am this, I must reach that." This is a necessary framework for the 'I' to continue and that is how the ego gets pampered. If nothing is there to be achieved and there are no psychological problems to be solved, the 'I' has no place and the ego will collapse. This is the fear that thought generates and the mind falls prey to it. The outcome: One looks for some method to hang on to so that one feels temporarily safe, and the 'I' digs itself into position.

Dissolution of the 'I' cannot take place through any effort of the 'I.' What brings about its end is pure awareness because such a witness attitude has no self-interest. One may ask, "How does this awareness begin?" This question can be answered by an attempted answer to another question, as follows.

Now, presumably, you are deeply interested in reading this book, especially if you have come this far. Many are not interested. How did this interest of yours come about? Was it the result of practicing a method or technique? No, it is the growing awareness in you that is already pushing you towards the Inner Being, perhaps without your notice. In other words, it is awareness that generates awareness and furthers itself. J. Krishnamurti's statement is relevant here: "Nothing brings in stillness except stillness."

When Ramana Maharishi tells us to embark on the quest "Who am I?" he is taking away our attention from "When will I achieve this?" to "Who is the achiever?" He does marginally recommend such things as observing one's breath but cautions the aspirant about becoming attached to such techniques. When a thing other than awareness can cause awareness, awareness becomes dependent on it; then that thing or another thing can destroy the awareness. Only when the awareness is its own cause, it is indestructible.

Buddha went through many practices and finally gave up everything and then suddenly the Cosmic Consciousness rushed into him. The significant thing here is the Buddha's own statement, "Nothing that I did or did not do had anything to do with this (Enlightenment)." Perhaps, it is good to go through the method-oriented approach in order to find for oneself that no method can help! If one can sense this early enough, one can avoid unnecessary struggles. In that state of complete non-action something takes place. It is a matter of total surrendering, without there being a 'surrenderer.'

As mentioned in chapter 4, if one's gut feeling tells one to adopt a method or technique, it may be good to go through it and give one's full attention to it. Simultaneously, it is healthy to watch one's mental disposition with regard to the achievement promised by the method. That way, even though one is on a method, awareness can flow in. Moving away from methods and techniques must happen spontaneously as a result of understanding and not through compulsion. If one turns away from methods as a matter of following a rule, then *not following any method* becomes the new method! One can approach these things with a sense of humor while being wary of the deceptive traps on the way.

In this book, an attempt is made to expose the reader to some obvious obstacles that stand in the way of transcending to the zone of freedom. It will be fun to watch these obstacles operate in us. After the initial exposure, one can carry on with the quest by oneself, through frequent reflections towards a progressive release from the noisy mind. That will put one on to a firm journey in the Esoteric Field. A few practical pointers towards sensing how the 'I' generates itself in the mind are given. These items cannot be molded into a technique. Since the whole thing is integrated with one's daily life, no separate time need be set up for any practice. Some periods of reflection will come into being naturally. They will happen spontaneously when the deeper call invites us and, therefore, we will not fall along any predetermined routine.

The Native Intelligence

Here we have to look into an industrial process known as *case-hardening*. This process involves hardening the surface of some components, such as machine tools, by impregnating carbon or other elements into the component's surface. It enhances the component's resistance to wear; that is the surface becomes harder. An important matter to be noted here is that the whole mass of the component is not treated but only its surface. In other words, the extraneous material like carbon enters only near the surface and makes it hard; the interior of the component remains soft.

Now we notice that our minds are also case hardened as we grow in age through contact with family, society, news media and the like. Conditioning factors impregnate our minds and harden the outer layers. Fortunately, as is the matter with industrial case-hardening, they can influence only the surface layers. Much of our interior Being remains unaffected. This understanding resonates with the item of Deep Ocean Peace that we saw in chapter 4.

One of the negative consequences of case-hardening on our minds is that we usually meet life through these hardened layers and make it unhappy for ourselves and others. Our responses bounce off from these surface layers rather than come out from our deeper being. Earlier in this book, this was referred to as the externalized state of mind. The full intelligence of our Being does not get a chance to be involved in the response. That unexpressed intelligence is what may be called the Native Intelligence because it is uncorrupted by the case-hardening process. When we begin to sense the hardened surface layers of our mind, we go deeper and feel the Native Intelligence. It has been knocking on our inner doors from our younger days but was rarely given a chance. Once we feel its unspoiled nature, we consult it more often and to that extent the case-hardened response diminishes. Confidence in life increases, not so much because of success but because of the inherent profundity that we sense in the Native Intelligence. This intelligence prevents us from leading a secondhand existence as a result of falling prey to religious and other propaganda. It alerts us to the point of avoiding endless repetition of what we are told and tutored to believe in. As mentioned before, group psychology differs from mob psychology only in degree, not in kind. The aloneness that characterizes the Esoteric Field helps us operate from our Native Intelligence.

The Natural Religion

An American soldier was hit by a bullet while he was in action in the Vietnam War of the seventies. During the surgical operation that followed, he died for about ten minutes as evidenced by his flat cardiac and cerebral signals. The change of consciousness that he felt during that near death experience (NDE) made him have abundant feelings for everything in life. Some days later, the hospital pronounced him fit to rejoin the army. He told his High Command that he could not kill anyone anymore and so he was useless to them as a fighter. After some investigation they found his statements to be plausible and so he was discharged and allowed to return to his country.

A person who functions from the naturally religious state has the same outlook and aliveness as someone who has had an NDE. Most people who go through NDE report a radical change, moving them towards positive and empathic attitudes. Some people have raised doubts to the effect that NDE may be nothing more than a dying brain's reaction and that it is just a kind of hallucination. However, hallucinations have never produced such long-standing and radical change in one's consciousness towards a holistic and compassionate outlook. The indelible impression and the transformation at the neurological level in the NDE-people are enough to establish the depth and value of that experience. Researchers say that the after-effects of NDE are the yardsticks for its authenticity (Atwater, 1989; Morse, 1992).

Abominable attachment to a religious system and sectarian practices can only divide people and bring about hatred, violence and war. Human dignity would be at stake. This sorry state of affairs can be changed only if each individual understands one's negative contribution to the collective consciousness in that respect.

The unimaginable harm perpetrated by man on animals for food, sports and research indicates an extremely irreligious state of the present-day human mind. Merely following a laid-out system and a set of rules in order to go to eternal heaven cannot make one a religious person. Being truly religious has to be seen in the depth of compassion one shows towards fellow beings, irrespective of whether they are human beings or animals, and irrespective of which religion or nation they belong to. A compassionate Jesus said, "Love thy neighbor as thyself." Obviously, this love has to be spontaneous and unconditional, independent of whether the other one belongs to one's own religion or not. If the neighbor is held in disdain because that person is a heathen, then love goes out of the window, not to the neighbor anyway! Outwardly, one may be goody-goody to that person but inwardly there would be alienation, and even ill will. This is, obviously, a clear case of hypocrisy.

In a person centered in Natural Religion, 'Love thy neighbor as thyself' takes place spontaneously because in that state one recognizes sacredness in all beings and manifestations. In it, man-made divisions have no meaning. It is to be noted here that nature too does not recognize man-made divisions.

The Primordial Fountain

From the above paragraphs, one can understand the freedom that prevails in the Esoteric Field as also the natural austerity. It may be described as freedom within orderliness and orderliness within freedom. A practical manifestation of this cyclic feedback between order and freedom can be found in the Indian Classical Music. For each *melodic mode* known as a Raga, there is a prescribed set of notes from an octave. This is a fixed order that controls a Raga. Within this order, the system provides infinite possibilities to render spontaneous combinations that sustain the raga's mood. Thus, there is order within which there is freedom but then there is another order within that freedom. This kind of cyclic feedback between mental order and freedom is what makes the Esoteric Field so healthy. The spontaneity of response has purity about it and that gives a primordial touch to the Esoteric Field.

Being natural, the mental state is one of deep relaxation. Whatever one does in that state will be right; that is it will be holistic and life-supportive. One no longer functions like a conformist. When such a mind expresses itself, it will have abundant feelings towards everyone. One can feel it flowing out like a fountain without one's volition. This is what is termed here as a Primordial Fountain.

When this happens, one sees the other person as the soul that the person is and not as the image that one has about that person. If we respond from the case-hardened state, we deal with a person through the mental residue that we have of that person from the past. This is harmful because the person is alive and the image is a dead thing! It is almost like treating living beings as dead entities! Having said this, can we treat the next person that we meet, a relative or a friend, as the soul that person is and not let our mental image of that person influence the interaction? This is an interesting experiment that we can conduct all the time. It creates an atmosphere of affection and laidback attitude. Quarrels pack up and leave.

When we are fully alive to the individuals we are interacting with, we do not let past and future play a role, except for factual information. That helps us bypass the mental image we have of them, our memory of how good or bad they are, what they did in the past and why they did what they did, where they are from, how they can be useful to us, and so on. It helps us interact without the conventional self-centered bent of mind that involves fear, regret, anger, desire and jealousy. Alert attention comes in with ease and functions naturally without effort. In short, when there is that aliveness, we *respond*, not *react*. Yes, let us keep clear in mind the difference between responding and reacting.

It is good to be alive to the fact that we are all sacred souls on a sacred journey. That would prevent us from being scared souls on a scary journey!

Chapter 6

The River as a Metaphor

A critical issue in life is to comprehend the larger context in which our individual life is transpiring. Life on this planet moves like a large flow in which we are all caught. Therefore, it is necessary to know how this flow affects us and how we can respond to it intelligently. The associated understanding brings about some inner transformation that frees us from being at the mercy of the flow. It helps us appreciate the deeper currents of life and sense something beyond the apparent. The river as a matter of water flow in a geographical context serves as an apt metaphor for the flow of our lives in an esoteric context. This aspect is explored in the present chapter.

At its source, the river is hardly noticeable. After some rivulets flow into each other, a mega-stream begins to take shape. Soon, a lot of water is collected and the waters pronounce themselves as a river. At this stage, it is usually on a mountain range, and so, rapids, torrents and waterfalls characterize the young river. Once the waters reach the plains, the serene and wide flow of the river is noticed for long distances. On flat areas, some miles before joining the sea, the force of the waters becomes weak and the river adopts a meandering flow. Finally, because of the low momentum, it starts depositing all the silt it brought from the mountains and the plains. The deposition causes some obstruction and so the waters divide themselves into a few branches, creating a delta area. Then the river quietly joins the sea. These various stages of the river can be likened to the youth, maturity and old age of human beings. Merger with the sea is similar to the individual consciousness merging with the wider consciousness when the body ends its course. However, this analogy is not the main purpose of the present chapter.

The Sankhya Philosophy

In order to bring in the actual metaphor, we have to look into what is known as the Sankhya Philosophy in the Indian heritage, expounded by Sage Kapila. He is one of the ancient sages of India. Sankhya is probably the first esoteric philosophy in the sense that it brought in a cosmological explanation to the interaction of matter and spirit. It postulates two primal interacting essences known as Purusha and Prakriti. Purusha is the unmanifest Divine essence that gives rise to consciousness and Prakriti is the manifest material universe with its laws of nature. Every living being in the universe is a spark of Purusha shrouded by Prakriti. That spark can be identified as the Athma (the Soul) familiar in our religious parlance. The spark when shrouded by Prakriti forgets its Divine essence. This causes the living being to assume an individual identity functioning with limited awareness. As the being evolves through the dynamic field of Prakriti, awareness grows and, firstly, leads to building up of the ego.

The level of awareness in the human being is deeper than that in animals and other living beings. This is what has helped man alter the environment to his advantage. However, it has been like a double-edged sword. On the one hand, it has helped man reduce dangers from nature and other sources but, on the other, he has destroyed animals and nature to his own detriment. His technological advancement has helped him in one way and has spelt death on the other. At the present stage of evolution, sufficient awareness has not entered the collective consciousness of man to let his intelligence help him live in harmony with himself, with his fellow beings and with his environment. This is where we come to grips with the root cause of the problem; it is a result of relying on the merely logical, circumferential approach and not paying attention to the Radial Dive, as outlined in chapter 4.

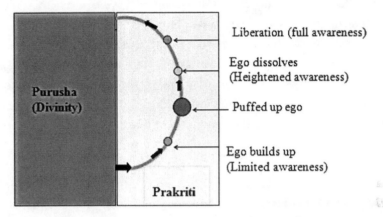

Fig. 8 Travel of the Divine Spark in Prakriti

In Fig. 8, the two primal factors, Purusha and Prakriti, are represented by two rectangles. The curved path in the field of Prakriti indicates the travel of the divine spark in the manifested field of Nature. At the beginning of the travel, partial awareness causes the ego to build up, as shown by the small circle. Individual consciousness owes its existence to this building up. 'I,' 'me' and the 'mine' are the results of this growth, and the ego begins to perform its circus. We notice that the stronger the ego, the farther the individual is from Divinity. Here, Jesus' parable of the Prodigal Son is relevant. At some stage, increasing awareness begins to enter the individual and starts dissolving the separate identity; that is the ego tends to become weaker and weaker. As evolution of consciousness in the individual progresses further, the ego is fully dissolved by the intensity of awareness; the spark becomes pure again, realizes its original nature and rejoins the source. The cycle is complete. Such is the mystical grandeur of the cosmological process functioning through the phenomenal universe and its variety of manifestations.

Carl Sagan, the well-known astrophysicist from the US, stated in his book *Cosmos* (Sagan, 2013) that the ancient wisdom of India had seen into the vast cosmological cycle of the universe extending to billions of years. He also remarked that only a cyclic process can be eternal, not something that begins at one end and ends at another. When we keep in mind such perspectives, our vista of awareness expands, and we go beyond the limited awareness of the conventional mind.

When the individual entity (arising out of partial awareness) traverses the field of Prakriti, the person is caught in the flow of nature governed by an extensive gamut of laws. Everything is linked in a subtle or gross way to everything else and nothing happens by chance. Things appear as random only because of limited awareness. A cause produces an effect which in turn becomes the cause of another effect, and so on. Thus, the link is pervasively set. The mind of the individual entity interacts with circumstances produced by Prakriti. It is this interaction that goes to make up our lives. Whether life is happy or unhappy is based on how well we understand the flow and how we guide it to help us, rather than being at crosscurrents with it.

It is interesting to note that the conversations Neale Donald Walsch had with God in the book *Tomorrow's God* (Walsch, 2004) reveal a Divine exposition that tallies amazingly with the ancient Sankhya philosophy. Chapter 6 of that book is particularly relevant.

The Similarity of a River and Prakriti

Now we look into the matter of a river being a metaphor for the flow of Prakriti.

Assume that a person is submerged and is moved along by the river flow. For the purpose of this analogy, we take it that he is going to remain submerged for quite some time. So let us give him an oxygen tank and make sure he doesn't drown! We also assume that he has been like this from his birth. Since water is all around him from the beginning, he can be quite unaware of the water itself. This is how we are unaware of the Prakriti's influence on us, being submerged in it from one's birth. The flow keeps moving the submerged person here and there, akin to Prakriti moving us through different circumstances. The river can take us along a smooth flow making us enjoy its buoyancy and the ride. Sometimes we get hit by rocks or get caught in the weeds and suffer. Similar situations in Prakriti are recognizable. With some understanding of the river flow, we can deflect ourselves by moving our limbs so that we don't get hit by the rocks or get entangled in the weeds. This reflects practical wisdom in our lives.

Most of us are functioning in this submerged situation. Some people effervesce as described in chapter 5 and bring their heads above the water surface. This is akin to entering the Esoteric Field. The scenario suddenly changes. One can see the river, its banks, stars, sky, clouds etc. We heave a sigh of relief and say, "So, this is what is happening!" The relief comes from the realization that there is a possibility of releasing ourselves from the force of the flow because we see that the flow zone is limited and it is only a part of the whole truth. We notice that there are many other things such as the shoals, trees, grass, and so on. We see that moving on to the banks, the flow can no longer affect us. In the submerged state, the mind's awareness of things is extremely limited. After we come above the surface, our awareness expands and correspondingly our perspective changes. Seeing the possibility of release, we wonder how to go to the banks. Through the heightened awareness, we learn to use our hands and feet properly, and navigate ourselves towards the shore. Eventually, we reach the banks and move over them. We are out of the river. This is Liberation. The liberated person is no longer affected by karma which is the essential factor in Prakriti. Outwardly, the person may appear to be affected by circumstances but that person's composure remains unaffected by those. The person is reunited with Divinity and is in bliss forever. Just as the person on the banks is free from the momentum of the river flow, the Enlightened person is free from the force of Prakriti.

The river has many messages to give, physically and metaphorically. To befriend a river is to befriend life. Understanding the river as a metaphor helps us in many ways, as outlined below:

1. We see that in the submerged state we have truly little control over our lives. Prakriti pushes us here and there and this makes us feel uneasy. With the application of wisdom, we bring about some order in our lives and do not easily buckle under adversity, not getting hit by the rocks or caught by the weeds in the river flow. However, an uncomfortable feeling remains because, subconsciously, we seem to know that there is such a thing like freedom, a state unaffected by Prakriti. This moves us to explore and discover what it means to bring our heads above the waters.

2. We understand that our fellow beings, the co-passengers on the journey of life, are also mostly submerged and suffering similar consequences. This leads to an empathic and compassionate outlook and we lend a helping hand to all those who need it. Because of this awareness, we complain less and adopt a more pardoning attitude.

3. When we bring our heads above the waters, we act as catalysts for the others to do the same. We also notice that some have gone ahead of us and we take their guidance in order to move to the banks.

4. Just as nature's great beauties are revealed after we come above the waters, a similar happening in the mental field is noticed. Our awareness expands beyond the conventional

rut into which human beings have fallen. This makes us gain a lot of trust in life and in the Unknown. Obviously, such trust leads to a peaceful life.

5. Once we are on the banks, we can always get into the waters whenever we want to because we know for sure how to return to freedom. This makes for complete confidence and the associated vibrant life. The analogy is that, after freedom, we can still play our roles in the ordinary life and not be at the mercy of Prakriti. We don't necessarily have to become a recluse for the reason that the mind is in a state of freedom.

It is noted in passing that bringing the head above the waters is analogous to rising above the Line of Transcendence in Fig. 7.

Chapter 7

The Noisy Mind

A great deal of our life is wasted by living on the surface of our consciousness. As we grow up from our young days, the compelling psychological atmosphere around us keeps us arrested on the surface. Unknowingly we all get caught in this whirlpool and, by the time we come to sense this, the habit has already gone very deep. The present human condition may be described as one thoroughly lost in the jumble of thought (or jungle of thought?!). Most people spend their whole life within the vortex of conditioned response and never go beyond the confines of a narrow, thought-created cage. The memory of the past overrules the present. This is the fundamental cause of unhappiness in life on this planet. An externalized state of mind provides the basis for fanaticism, vindictive attitudes, depression, boredom, persecution complex, loneliness, and many other undesirable mental states. Those who are reflective realize this with a shock and wonder how to release themselves from the tyranny of this mental state. Simultaneously, they feel that the externalized state of mind has made them move away from their deeper self. In other words, there is a sense of impoverishment of the soul. Sadly, as mentioned before, the externalization continues in the field of religion too. That is why the ego plays a significant role in those practices and there are the exclusivist attitudes, divisions and conflicts in the name of religion. Religious activities also seem to fall within the same confines of self-importance created by thought. As Nisargadatta Maharaj (Dikshit, 1973) put it, the lust for heaven is no different from the lust for physical pleasures. They both arise out of the ego's self-centered activity. It is the same thing if Enlightenment becomes an object of desire, as then the ego takes hold of it.

Thus, overall, the noisy mind has a stranglehold on the vast majority of people.

Earlier, in chapter 4, we looked into the item of mentation. That state is truly relevant to the discussion of the noisy mind.

As soon as we get up in the morning, we can see how quickly thought captures our mental state and keeps us under its thumb until we go to sleep at night. This continuous neuron movement controlled by the image that each one has about oneself wears out the mind, leading to an unhealthy mindset. Certain things help us see how this process keeps us trapped in its vortex. These are explained in the present chapter for the reader's reflection and sensing. Clarity on those items can make us come to grips with the situation and do something about it, even though it sounds like a losing battle at the beginning. This movement is initially arduous because one has to sail an uncharted sea and be a guide unto oneself. External guidance can only be of some inspirational value.

Now we go into an exploration of the noisy mind. It helps us bring about some clarity and can be a good forerunner for the inner dive to set in. Causal factors for the mind to be noisy are sensed in the following analyses.

The Conditioning Elements

Environmental conditioning: As the child grows in the atmosphere of its family and society, two primary emotions govern the child's psychology, namely *desire* and *fear*. This coupled with the fact that people around are already functioning in a conditioned state results in the child's mind being pulled into the vortex of similar conditioning. Even when the child rebels against it, perhaps as a teenager, it succeeds only in producing a counterconditioning; it does not steer itself to freedom. This has been the human situation for thousands of years.

There are two other factors, subtler than the one considered above.

Genetic conditioning: The neurological factors that worked in the minds of one's forefathers (and 'foremothers' too!) get transmitted to the child and influence the child's thinking. The immediate parents' traits are noticeable in most children but traits can even follow skipping some generations. Genetic conditioning is responsible for many of the neurological responses and that is why J. Krishnamurti points to it as a centuries-old habit.

Past-life conditioning: The soul carries with it memories of past lives in connection with the individual's psychological evolution. This also influences thought at the neurological levels. The Divine Voice in *Conversations with God* (Walsch, 1995) says that the soul conceives, the mind creates and the body experiences. Elsewhere in that book, the Divine Voice confirms the truth of reincarnation.

Apart from the three major types mentioned above, there may be other factors such as climate, geography and the like that contribute to the mental conditioning. Thus, we see that this matter of conditioned response from an individual is quite a complex matter. When we remember this in dealing with people, we will treat them with sympathy rather than be too judgmental about them. One of Jesus' statements is relevant here: Forgive them for they know not what they are doing.

These things make it clear that there is such a thing as a psychological content for each person. This is referred to as the Mental Content in this book. Each one responds to life's circumstances from it. The mental residue that leads to emotional image formation is an essential aspect of that content. Even though this content gets modified by one's experiences in life, one characteristic of it remains the same: It is quick and jumps to the front in meeting circumstances. This implies that the past plays a significant role in determining a person's reactions.

That brings us to the question: Where does free-will come into all this? The only psychological state that is free and untouched by the past is the simple self-awareness. It is the state of mind referred to earlier as the noninterfering witness. That alone is free from being influenced by the Mental Content of a person. All the Enlightened Masters have emphasized this point. When that aliveness is there, the content's reaction is modified and one's response is imbued with compassion rather than be controlled by the past. To think that free-will implies that one can take any decision one wants, uninfluenced by one's Mental Content, is to be ignorant of the secret powers of the residues from the past. Those who have sensed the content's power know that it is a juggernaut. As J. Krishnamurti says, "It is much too quick for you to control." Thus, the only thing that can dissolve its power is an action in the present, namely, the quiet self-awareness that is uninfluenced by the past. The joy of self-awareness clears the obstacles for more intense awareness to step in. Thus, if by free-will we mean a state in which thinking is rooted in self-awareness, then there is freedom from the influence of past residues. When we take decisions, the power and influence of psychological residues go unnoticed unless there is self-awareness of sufficient depth.

In Sanskrit, the phrase 'Gunas of Prakriti' is often used. This phrase means 'characteristics of the flow of nature.' Krishna says in the Gita, "In all cases, Arjuna, actions are done by the Gunas of Prakriti, but he whose mind is deluded by egoism thinks 'I am the doer.' We see that this delusion is the same that makes one think, 'I am the one who is taking decisions.'"

Introspective Analysis, not useful: When we are confronted with a problem or challenge, the usual tendency is to enter into a mentally generated verbal analysis known as introspection. It does help us in dealing with the practical matters associated with the problem and so, in that respect, it becomes a necessity. However, beyond that it only encourages the habitual thought because it prevents us from listening to the deeper self, which alone can bring about a wholesome solution. As a result, the endless chattering leads to a noisy mind. A 'reflect and reject' kind of approach can be helpful in letting silence prevail over the matter after the practical aspects are considered and decisions made. We must be aware of the fact that thought fragments reality and cannot bring the fragments together to perceive the matter in the context of the whole. With proper understanding, we distrust introspective analysis except for practical aspects. We then move into the stillness that is ever waiting for us like an affectionate mother behind the thought realm. True intelligence becomes operative in a silent mind. Solutions to problems pop up from the inner stillness.

In regard to the mind's invitation to indulge in analysis, Ramana Maharishi warns us: "It behaves like a good friend but slowly pushes you down a deep pit!" Another Master echoes, "Search for an answer through the mind leads nowhere." At best, it can be palliative. It attempts to give us some comfort, like a painkiller for a headache. The headache will soon recur because the root of the problem is not removed. Later, we will see that the root lies in our assumption that the thought-created 'I' is an independent entity. That it is merely a product of thought and that it has no intrinsic substantiality are not easily perceived. This illusion is at the source of all problems. The Masters tell us that the real Self or the real 'I am' is untouched by thought and that the thought-created 'I' is an imposter. People who go through a near death experience feel that fact while being submerged in the other reality. That we are unaware of this in the ordinary state of mind is the fundamental malady.

Psychological Identifications: The mental habit is to create an image of oneself through some identification such as nationality, race, religion, language, political ideology and the like. There are subtler images, such as the gender identity, that function at hard-to-perceive deeper levels. The True Self has no gender. Without some form of identification, the ego cannot subsist. Each one of these identifications creates a knot as mentioned in paradigm 2 of chapter 4. Vortices are generated in the thought field by the identifications and they make the mind noisy.

In general, eight forms of thought vortices can be recognized as the main source of noise in the mind. Self-awareness brings us to our understanding of how these vortices operate.

The Eight Vortices

During the waking hours, the mind is usually caught in thought vortices and this causes the mind to remain occupied. Those vortices are of eight types in general. It is suggested that the reader looks into this critically and modifies the analysis wherever scope arises. Such applications can make matters interesting and bring in clarity.

The five major vortices are:

1. Fear and Anxiety
2. Anger and Hatred
3. Regret and Sadness
4. Desire and Greed
5. Self-pity and Jealousy

The three minor ones are:

1. Megalomania
2. Rehearsal
3. Inadvertence

The major vortices are self-explanatory. They are given here as pairs, the second in each pair being the stronger of the two. Those mentioned as minor vortices deserve some explanation.

If we have done something in a nice way, the mind goes over it again and again in the form of "How nicely I did it!" It feels good to the ego. Megalomania is this kind of high feeling about oneself. Sometimes, it may involve imaginary scenarios too, such as being a winner in a game, a humorous speaker in a group and the like. The thought-created phantasmagoria is responsible for the vortex of megalomania.

Rehearsals involve scenes of the future where we have to deal with somebody either in harmony or in disharmony with us. An anticipated business deal, quarrel, or a friendly get-together in the near future can trigger it. Such rehearsals may have a meaningful practical side to them. That does not allow thought to capture us and so does not do any harm. It is the image-oriented thought process (based on self-importance) that forms the harmful vortex. It traps us in unawareness.

Inadvertence is the lazy flitting from one thought to the next merely driven by habit. While traveling by a bus, for example, the passing scenes or signboards may trigger this wasteful thought process. In a way, such situations give us an opportunity to understand how we get drawn in by the habitual neurology.

Of the eight vortices mentioned above, the major ones push us into deeper unawareness and so into deeper harm than the minor ones. They affect our lives significantly. In any case, all the eight vortices are primarily responsible for the externalization of our minds. They take place in unawareness and, in turn, strengthen the unawareness. Once we begin to sense this, awareness begins to take over.

It can be a curious exercise to attempt to understand what happens when, through our awareness, we remain untouched by the eight vortices during our waking hours. What transpires then takes us into the region that Eckhart Tolle often exhorts us to visit through his book *Stillness Speaks* (Tolle, 2003). By the way, this book is a classic on Athma Vichara (Soul Search).

Sometimes identification with a spiritual or religious system may make one feel that one is free of the ego. In so far as there is identification, the ego will use it to its end and, in such cases as these, it usually hides behind a mask of respectable facade. That is what may be called *the pious ego*! It is deceptive. Explicit ego, the well-known one that throws its weight around, is easily recognized, but it is not easy to notice the pious ego. Explicit ego is like a tiger. Yes, it is dangerous, but the pious ego is like a tiger in cow's skin; more dangerous! One has to be wary of giving room to this dubious tenant in one's mind.

Self-importance is what causes one to chase something in the so-called spiritual world. Self-awareness brings us to the point of understanding the absurdity behind such self-centered chases; one then gives up the chase and begins to look in. This is very much like Jesus' parable of the Prodigal Son. The son goes away, away and away, and then, seeing the absurdity of it, returns home. The Masters say that because of the inwardly turned attention in oneself, the Radial Dive sets in, the cloud is cleared and the Truth revealed.

The Thought-Sphere

There is a general feeling that thinking is entirely originated from within us and that oneself is the sole author of it. This is only partly true. The hidden side of it comprises a thought continuum that some Masters term as the thought-sphere, like the atmosphere around us. One's mind resonates with the vibrations in that sphere, very much like a radio picking up signals from a field of waves generated by a broadcast. The antenna that our mind puts up depends on the individual and we pick up exactly only those vibrations that resonate with our individual Mental Content. When we become aware of this, we can see the bombardment from outside on our thought formations.

Because of the thought-sphere influence, most of the ideas and concepts that we carry with us have been given to us by others. Identifying oneself with them gives one a feeling of satisfaction and security. From the many influences, we pick up those that click with our conditioning as explained earlier. Such a situation compels us to be secondhand human beings. The surreptitious capturing of one's consciousness by society is one of the main reasons for our unawareness. Remaining alert, we can sense the vibrations entering from outside and so we can keep them off. If we notice that a rat has come into our house, before we wish to chase it away, we ask how it came in. We must block the possibility of reentry before we think of sending out the intruder. The same way, we must understand how the thought-sphere enters us before we apply ourselves to ejecting its influence.

This thing brings us to the point of understanding how we get woven into the psychological fabric of society and so find it difficult to release ourselves from it. There is a practical need to be in touch with that fabric, and in the process we fall prey to the thought-sphere. This is where we have to apply discrimination and be alert enough not to let the rat in. At the beginning, the stranglehold that the psychological fabric of society has over us is hard to perceive. Its effect can be seen in the way people have given themselves over to the media. Newspapers, magazines, radio, TV and the Internet severely grip people's daily consciousness and effectively thwart their self-awareness. But that in itself can serve as a blessing in disguise because it gives us a chance to sense how the thought-sphere influences us. Mental pollution by the media is a pertinent factor; it is good to be aware of if we are to appreciate the beauty of the Esoteric Field.

Contemporary Thought: This is a principal issue while considering the noisy mind. What goes on around us in society as intellectual issues involving controversies captures our attention and, unknowingly, we get threaded into that fabric. We lose ourselves in that noise to the point of being unaware of our True Self. Quite often, that stream of contemporary thought appears to be significant while it is nothing more than conditioned thinking. When we see its empty nature, it becomes easy to release ourselves from it.

Contemporary thought is also influenced by history as memory. Human beings caught in contemporary thought behave like dolls in a puppet show, entities controlled by external forces. Self-awareness makes us step out of the fabric and we heave a sigh of relief, we cease to be puppets.

Here we ask: Can one run one's daily life as if our body is here but the mind is in a period four hundred years ago, except for practical matters? Or four hundred years hence? That helps us free ourselves from the poison of contemporary thought. Calm association with the flow of life becomes possible. The mind is at rest. An interesting thing about it is that this release from contemporary thought takes place spontaneously during a near death experience (NDE) and sometimes during the convalescent period after a serious illness. It also happens when people are terminally ill and know that they are going to die soon. That is why death-bed utterances have been known to be profound and away from conditioned thinking. Now the question is: Can one release oneself from the tyranny of contemporary thought without requiring a crisis situation to bail one out? The Esoteric Field provides answers to such questions.

In matters of esoteric interests, however, one may consider what different people are saying in order to zero in on the actuality. In such cases, an approach that may be termed Mutually Exclusive Multiple Pointers (MEMP), explained later in chapter 9, may be found interesting and useful. Tempered skepticism is the guide. Elusive issues like the NDE and Reincarnation provide good grounds for exploration by the MEMP approach.

In 1989, a Kuwaiti newspaper reported the demise of the Iranian Head of State at that time, Ayatollah Khomeini, who was severe on his adversaries. The Ayatollah was terminally ill and, about ten days before his end came, he stopped talking. However, two or three days before he passed away, he said a few words in a weak voice to his grieving relatives. "Life on this planet is hard. All you can do is to make sure that you don't make too many mistakes." were those words. His deathbed utterance has esoteric implications.

The Outer Self

The outer self is the psychological medium through which a human being interacts with the world. In computer language, it would be called the interface between one's Inner Being and the world. The outer self is characterized by the Mental Content engendered by the environmental, the genetic and the past-life conditioning. Behind the outer self is the uncorrupted Being characterized by Universal Consciousness, that which has neither a beginning nor an ending. This Being is the source of awareness. When awareness issues out through the outer self, as a matter of stifled outlet, there is the conditioned response of the human being. Because the three types of conditioning mentioned above can have infinite variations, their combination makes each human being a unique character. This uniqueness calls for the respect that each person deserves.

As awareness deepens, it begins to dissolve the Mental Content, thereby allowing the Inner Being to permeate one's daily life. When this process is complete, the Mental Content does not interfere except in purely practical affairs, and we say that the human being is in a state of Enlightenment. It is then that the illusion of being a separate individual (that is the ego) vanishes. Long before the process is complete, the human being begins to feel the impact of the Inner Being in daily life. However, the effect is not easily seen in the worldly behavior of a human being for quite a while, because the Mental Content continues to hold sway by its tremendously wound state. One's outlook in daily life changes when one becomes aware of the Mental Content's centuries-old momentum. We tend to be less disturbed by other's faults and shortcomings, and by our own too.

The outer self is habit ridden and habit driven. From the age of two or three, it begins to get wound by mental movements governed by limited awareness. It goes on getting wound as the days pass by and begins to obliterate the pure awareness springing from the Inner Being. This is what ends up in creating the crystallized image we have about ourselves and others. This thought-created, hardened image that one assumes oneself to be is the basis for all suffering. To release one's mind from the tyranny of this image is not easy. Fortunately, it is not impossible. To be able to see this state of affairs and wonder at the slavery of the mind to the Mental Content is already an indication to show that the ground-breaking ceremony is over! It is fun to watch the awareness function in its own way as it proceeds to clear the ground. All we have to do is to take our hands off and be an interested bystander. Any attempt to bring in a formula or a method in order to free oneself from the image proceeds from the outer self and so can only serve to bolster that self. In contrast, passive awareness has great potency. As the phrase itself shows, passive awareness cannot be put into the framework of a practice. This is because practices are result-oriented, and so, not passive! All one can do is to understand the beauty of passive awareness and leave it alone. It furthers itself.

When we are on a long bus journey, it gives us a chance to see how the outer self keeps us under its thumb during our waking hours. Watching it capture our attention is fun. We may feel we are alert enough, but it is so tricky that suddenly we find that it has had us trapped for a while. During the journey, this game of being alternatively attentive and inattentive goes on for some time but soon we sense mental quietude settling down and the outer self rendered inoperative. A hollow state of mind prevails. We enjoy the passing scenes, hear the steady hum of the tires and note many other things that take place in the Now. We watch other passengers and see what is going on in the bus. The alert attention of the driver controlling the speeding bus is something to watch. Most people are lost in thought and some are dozing off. However, the self-awareness in us prevailing during the journey brings about a quiet mind; it can continue to keep us company even after getting off the bus!

Religious practices do help in a minor way towards self-awareness but soon they themselves become obstructive to the process of clearing the Mental Content because they aim at feeding the ego. Freedom from the ego is not in the interest of religious practices, even though they may say they are praying for the whole of mankind. That is clearly a case of pious egoism!

A word of caution is necessary here. Even though we talk of the Inner Being and the outer self, there are no two isolated selves and there is no hard and fast division between them. They belong to a continuum. At one end of the continuum is the Inner Being and at the other the outer self. Take, for example, a bar magnet. It has a north pole and a south pole but they belong to one piece of iron even though they are poles apart! Between the two poles is a neutral zone. Perhaps, such a thing exists between the Inner Being and the outer self too. This may be the vacuous state that one feels at the beginning when moving into the Esoteric Field. It is because, at that time, one sees the need to give up everything that one has accumulated psychologically while one has not yet begun to feel the compassionate embrace of the Inner Being.

The Human Violence

The primary reason for human violence is the noisy mind. This violence ranges from simple quarrel between two people to war between countries. Mankind has seen tremendous suffering due to antagonism. Yet, continues to wallow in the same games in spite of the fact that Masters, religious leaders and pacifists have attempted to expose people to the beauty of compassion and bonhomie. We have lived for several thousand years on this planet but human violence has remained unabated. Now, each one of us has a role to play in bringing about a peaceful and caring society. During a talk given in 1970 in India, J. Krishnamurti said, "Do you know, Sirs, that you are responsible for the war in Vietnam, though sitting here in Chennai?" The conventional mind would see no meaning in this. This is where the thought-sphere mentioned above comes into the picture.

There are many books that graphically depict human violence and the untold suffering that human beings have gone through as a result. One of them is by Jacobo Timerman titled *Prisoner without a name, Cell without a number* (Timerman, 1981). The following is summarized from the cover presentation of that book.

Jacobo, the Argentine newspaper publisher who dared to criticize his government's policy of cruel repression, tells the horrifying story of his arrest, imprisonment and torture before he was released in 1979 by a worldwide campaign against the atrocity. With no charges brought against him, he was held captive for thirty months, and barbarously tortured and interrogated about his loyalty to Argentina, to which he had come as a child, from the Soviet Union. In September 1979, he was expelled from Argentina after a harrowing experience of his trip to the airport. Timerman's book conveys the anguish and desperation he endured as a prisoner: How it felt to be tortured and locked in isolation, with only an occasionally open peephole as his companion. Through unswerving passivity and capacity to endure, he managed to preserve his sanity in spite of a torment that could have spelt total breakdown to many. The last few lines with which he ends his book are indeed poignant.

In those lines he asks whether any of us have ever looked into the eyes of a person on the cell floor who suspects that he may be executed. That person feels he may be close to death but, prompted by a lingering hope, clings to his desire to live. Timerman says that many such gazes have been imprinted upon him while he was in prison. Those gazes, which he encountered in the prisons of Argentina and which remained deeply etched in his memory, were the saddest part of his tragedy. He says that, even if he wished to do so, he could not and would not know how to share them with us.

It is to be noted that Argentina is not alone in this. Violence has been rampant in all countries throughout history.

If that be so regarding man against man, the situation is even worse with regard to the harm perpetrated by man on animals. If you are truly a religious person and consider spirituality as an essential part of your life, you cannot but apply yourself to the ending of suffering to animals by man. The book titled *Animal Liberation* by Peter Singer (Singer, 1990) is a classic in this respect, among other publications. It is indeed a very spirited book where the author has not only critically analyzed all the harm imposed on animals but also poured forth his heart in his appeal to humanity to move to saner grounds by considering animals as brethren. He quotes Voltaire in a chapter as follows:

There are barbarians who seize this dog which so greatly surpasses man in fidelity and friendship, and nail him down to a table and dissect him alive, to show you the Mesaraic veins! You discover in him all the same organs of feeling as in yourself. Answer me, mechanist, has nature arranged all the springs of feeling in this animal to the end that he might not feel?

It is interesting to note that, in another chapter, he develops a strong case for vegetarianism through the twin issues of human health and avoidance of animal suffering.

If you have already reflected on the atrocities unleashed by man on animals, it would be good to go through Peter Singer's book. The psychological intensity of the resulting feeling can bring about redemption of some kind in its own way.

Chapter 8

The Radical Transformation

We have so far considered several factors that point to a noisy mind and the associated unawareness. Reflections on those and the related applications can bring about confidence in our daily lives. It is a matter of combining seriousness with nonchalance, even though these two appear contradictory to each other. A hodgepodge mixture of the two is not what is meant but an intelligent and harmonious blending of them. This challenge itself can be very educative.

The Radical Transformation of the human mind towards inner silence and tranquility is not easily brought about because we are not trained to look at it from our young days. In fact, from childhood everything around us takes us away, exactly in the opposite direction. It does not mean that the difficulties are insurmountable. All it implies is that phenomenal patience is required, as also sustained interest in that direction. Looking for quick results will lead to disappointments. In fact, one has to turn entirely away from the result-oriented approach. Very soon we realize that such a transformation is its own reward. Since it transpires from deep within, it may take quite a while before it begins to show its impact on one's outer behavior. By that time, we are not really concerned about what others think about us; the usual preoccupation with one's self-image is on the way out. As soon as we begin to pay attention to this matter, we feel as though we are in the driver's seat of our life's journey. The intrinsic beauty of the transformation keeps us on its tracks and reminds us that just living vibrantly every day brings on goodness in the lives of oneself and others.

An important thing to be noted here is that such a transformation is not aimed at making one 'perfect' or a 'good person.' This may sound strange because we are told, by everyone around, to become a virtuous person, to have ideals and so on. Such things are directed towards enhancing one's image and it will meet with ready approval by one's people and society. As the image is the ego's prime instrument, motivations like chasing an ideal are clearly sponsored by the ego. It is not suggested that we be wayward or footloose but that we must be wary of pious egoism and its tricky invitations. While its designs are grandiose, it will only serve to keep us arrested in unawareness by focusing our attention on polishing the image. Take for example a person who wants to become humble because humility is a virtue and it is nice for oneself to be called a humble person. After some practice, the person may feel that he is the humblest person around! This lands one exactly on the opposite ground! That is, chasing an ideal serves only to feed the ego. This raises the question as to how humility comes into being at all. Awareness of arrogance is a movement of humility. Awareness is a fundamental virtue and, when it is there, all other virtues fall in place. Thus, humility comes in as a by-product of self-awareness, and then it doesn't get embroiled with the ego.

Predetermined methods and techniques cannot bring about Radical Transformation, the reason being that they are rooted in the past. When the past colors the present *'Being in the Now'* becomes obstructed. Usually, the methods aim at the 'achiever' getting the 'achieved' in the future. The 'Now' becomes a mere passage. Sustenance of such a duality as the 'achiever' and the 'achieved' is what puts forth the psychological time and so we will be back to square one where the ego rules the roost. Those who rely on methods sense some achievement after a while and feel thrilled about it. Sooner or later, they find that the core has remained the same. Whatever happened was no more than a scratch on the surface. When this is understood, there is a movement away from all methods directed towards some spiritual gain; the mind becomes quiet in a state of non-action. The ego feels stifled by this quietude. There is no struggle any more to reach some predetermined goal. In that state of mind, Radical Transformation begins of its own accord.

Fundamental transformation is to be triggered by our interest in discovering what lies behind and beyond the apparent. Such a quest may be called Athma Vichara or Soul Search. Here we once again recall the age-old adage, "Know thyself." This cannot be in the interest of the ego, as the quest does not enhance the image of oneself. In fact, it will be seen as a threat to the image, and so the ego will do everything to discourage such an approach. Some religious people may even go so far as to say that those approaches are invitations by the devil! When we notice that an inwardly directed quest has its impact on our perception and serves to clear our ignorance, we are reminded of a Buddha's statement, "The prime cause of human suffering is ignorance." The noisy mind, which is essentially a state of unawareness, is the one that feeds the ego and is the chief culprit in sustaining the ignorance.

When we observe that every effort of the mind to reach freedom (or peace) reaches a dead end, there is a natural suspension of all movements of the mind except those for purely practical purposes. It is good to sense that state of total helplessness as it is a prelude to Radical Transformation. It is tantamount to total surrendering as a natural accompaniment. Usually, the mind hangs on to some religious or other avenues and thwarts that state of total abnegation. It is a state of uncomfortable emptiness which the noisy mind dislikes. To remain in that state is not easy. It is like trying to balance a ball on the top of a cone. It easily slips down. Similarly, proclivity of the mind is to move away from that uneasy state, driven by the gravity of habitual thought. When the value of non-action is made clear through self-awareness, one sees its beauty and does not roll out from that apparent emptiness. Thought can no longer play its tricks. The mind lies fallow in that state of passivity. It is a potential state in which something new can be born, like a primordial spring, untouched by the past.

In a talk given by J. Krishnamurti at the Ommen Camp Fire Talks (Krishnamurti, 1927), he said, "There lies the greatness of the moment, for there be very few days of summer, days when you can gather in your hay, when you can prepare your house and put all things in order to welcome the Guest." Thus, this metaphor indicates that we can only remain open for the Truth to arrive as the Guest. We cannot drag the Guest in!

Now we look into some practical moments in daily life. We recall that at the end of chapter 3, we got off the train after reaching the terminus. Then, we look for a local transport, such as a taxi or an autorickshaw. As one moves on by that vehicle, what is the state of one's mind? It is usually caught up in some item of anxiety to be attended to soon after reaching one's residence. Or the mind is lazily flitting from one thought to the next. Is one aware of the vehicle's driver, a living being sitting not too far from us? Some of these drivers are neatly dressed and maybe wearing an impressive wristwatch. In contrast, some indicate neglected self-care. Do we notice the driver at all or are we just sunk in our own thoughts to the point of being totally oblivious of the other human being sitting next to us? Is he just a means to our end? If we do notice him and indulge in conversation, we find quite often that, notwithstanding his minimal education, he comes up with intelligent statements. Perhaps, his unspoiled, native intelligence is at work!

During the above-mentioned travel, we may be accompanied by a relative or a friend, sitting next to us. Can we look at that person as if for the first time and not let our image about that person interfere? And then, are we aware of the vehicle itself and the fact that it has a life of its own? Is the mind in quiet communion with all the things that transpire around one during the travel? When we notice the state of our own minds, Radical

Transformation takes place in an unobtrusive way. It begins at some unknown depths in us and quietly moves towards the periphery.

While this slipping smoothly into *what is* does not require any precondition, it does take place due to our interest in discovering the deep ocean calmness within us. We would rather not care for that inner zone if things were 'going our way.' In this connection one is reminded of a cute poster that some of us would have seen. The colorful picture depicts some hunters on horseback along with a bunch of dogs running with them. They seem to be thrilled and well set on their mission. The caption says, "If everything is going your way, you are probably heading the wrong way!" Does that mean that if things are going wrong, we are heading the right way?! Maybe not, but at least they make us stop and reflect. In that sense, the unacceptable circumstances are a blessing because they usher in self-awareness and give us a push towards the deep ocean calmness. When we combine this interest with efficiency in practical matters, we bring in a healthy state that makes us swim serenely amidst the turbulent waters of life.

People in whom Radical Transformation has started taking place do not manipulate life to fit their egoistic demands. They let life flow through them like breeze through the trees. At the same time, they do not dilute their sincerity in practical applications; nor do they shrink from enjoying the good things that come uninvited.

One adopts an affectionate bystander attitude. It is like running at the same speed as life does, and so being in complete harmony with it. If two trains are running on parallel tracks with the same speed in the same direction, the view of one from the other is very clear; there is no blur. This is what happens if we can move at the same speed as that of life's flow.

We are aware of the fact that self-awareness cannot be practiced through a formula. It has to happen naturally and spontaneously, as a result of our interest in that direction. Certain things, however, can act as catalysts to the process of Radical Transformation. The catalysts are discussed below. They are not to be practiced as methods but must be allowed to happen at their own times because of our seeing their potential. In other words, they happen because of one's understanding and not as a result of one's effort.

The Bardo

There are times during our daily lives when our consciousness is not obscured by thought. With the noisy mind in action, such moments are few and far between. However, there are two occasions during the day when consciousness is less obscured by mental noise. On those occasions, there is a gap across which the mind jumps so quickly that we don't notice the pure awareness existing in that gap. These are the moments immediately after waking up in the morning and those just before falling asleep. During those very short periods, consciousness shifts from sleep to waking and the other way. Called *Sandhyakal* in Sanskrit, they represent the meeting place of two things in time, and, in Tibetan language, it is called Bardo. When we bring ourselves to focus on these Bardo periods, we get an inkling of pure awareness, a state of mind that is not dominated by thought. During our young days, the Bardo is somewhat long but, as we grow up, it shrinks thin to a tenth of a second or even less. Fortunately, it can never be reduced to zero. In the mornings, we can see how the thought-surge invades us as soon as we are awake. It is good to observe this thought entry as it takes place and see how long one can remain in pure awareness. After some time, it becomes relatively easy to stay in Bardo long enough to appreciate its silence. Then it begins to keep company with us through the day. The second Bardo, in the night, is a time when it is relatively harder to keep up one's alertness. However, it becomes viable with continued interest. Such awareness clears a burdened state of mind before falling asleep and so our sleep is likely to go deeper. In other words, the quality of sleep improves and there is the likelihood of fewer dreams and less disturbing ones at that; it would be a salutary by-product.

Here, we note the pointers from some Masters. They direct our attention to the gap between two happenings; such as the gap between two gongs of a bell, the tiny lull between the in-breath and the out-breath, the gap when one song ends and the other is about to begin. We can also pay attention to the silence that follows the last patter of rain on the roof or the one that ensues at the abrupt stopping of an air conditioner. Those moments invite us to look into the formless consciousness that provides the platform for everything to dance on.

The Shattering Readings

If we read a story or poem, it may move us to be pensive, especially if it has a touch of melancholy. It may shatter the psychological mold that we cling to. The same thing can happen through a movie. Human suffering can be a good starting point for the inward dive. Happy tidings that transpire in those readings can also serve the same purpose. It would be appropriate to reflect on those pointers and allow deeper understanding to move in.

One must differentiate between reflection and introspection. While reflection is supported by awareness, introspection proceeds by questions and answers; the former is driven more by intuition and the latter by the intellect. Introspection can be enervating and does not take us along the Radial Dive described in chapter 4. We discover our deeper being through reflections. It helps us bring about mental quietude and a maturity that ushers in calmness. Many people indulge in such reflections but not in a sustained way. It proceeds well for some time but soon tapers off and gets lost in the busy crowding-in of life. A few friends and relatives may show interest in those penetrative reflections and it is obviously good to involve ourselves in discussions with them. The synergy in group involvement is a positive force. Depending on their interest in the esoteric aspects of life, such interactions can function as catalysts to the Radial Dive in all those involved.

Going through books depicting talks of some Masters can also produce shattering readings. This is because such talks tend to demolish the mental wall that we build around us through the noisy mind. The shattering feeling is particularly evident when our pet conclusions come under attack. They strike away all the moorings we cling to via attachments to belief systems and the like. Those moorings provide a false sense of security. Total surrender can take place only when all that the ego relies on is dissolved. Being cut off from the moorings that appear to uphold our security, one may feel very disturbed. If we do not fall for such disturbances and continue to maintain our interest in the inward journey, we soon fall into a new mental rhythm. That brings in truer security through a deeper order. Shattering readings are like the proverbial surgeon's knife; they open the gates for the Inner Being to penetrate our outer consciousness. Consequently, self-awareness keeps us company during our waking hours, sponsoring a serene state of mind. Compassion expresses itself in our interactions spontaneously.

Reflections on OBE

Over the past several decades, research has been conducted on the *Out-of-Body Experience* (OBE). The individual's consciousness leaves the body and moves on to a nearby or distant zone while that person's body remains at a given location. Limitations of the body are transcended and the consciousness feels unburdened from the conditioned brain. Many authentic accounts have been collected by researchers and published for the sake of the esoterically inclined readers. Those who understand the value of Radical Transformation will find this topic very absorbing. A good publication in this respect, among others, is *Leaving the*

Body by D. Scott Rogo (Rogo, 1983). That book talks about Dr. Raynor Johnson collecting details on many cases of OBE and the associated peak feelings. The following is summarized from an exhilarating account supplied to Dr. Johnson by one of his correspondents. For the sake of explanation let us give that correspondent a pseudonym: Mr. Henry Craze!

It was 11 pm on a night in October. Henry found himself out of his body floating over an expansive wasteland. He felt very light and noticed such things as the woods on the land and clouds drifting past the moon. As he floated along, he felt a cool breeze flow past him. He would have felt uneasy by the coldness if he were to be in his body, but now he did not mind the wind because he felt he was at one with it. (There was no duality as 'feeler' and 'the felt.') A comprehensive sensing made him feel that the life in the wind, the clouds and the trees were within him too. Glorious life filled him. He experienced a state of timelessness and so he could not tell whether that experience lasted many minutes or only a few seconds.

Henry came back greatly rejuvenated by the ravishing experience. In the aftermath, a strange thought occurred to him: If this is the beatitude that the so-called dead experience, how much more vitally alive they are than we feel here!

Satori and NDE

Radical Transformation of our minds leads to freedom of consciousness even while being associated with a body. In this connection, Appendices 1 and 2 give accounts by those who experienced Satori, mentioned in chapter 4. It is good to see parallels and differences between an OBE and Satori experience. This exercise is left to the reader.

As indicated by those experiences, the mind undergoes a purging of all egoistic accumulations in the form of 'I,' 'me' and the 'mine.' That catharsis is a profound experience. As you see in Appendix 3, Kurt Friedrichs says that such experiences did not arise as a result of his own volition but rushed at him without control leaving an indescribable happiness behind them. One can see that this is something like an abyssal collapse of all thought forms and the tyranny of attachment to people, things and beliefs. Clinging to such forms is what makes our death so fearful. As mentioned before, many near death experiences (NDEs) have shown a similar state of affairs; they indicate that consciousness can exist independent of the body. NDE people report the same ravishing experience that makes their ego absent while the experience lasts. They are transformed into beings who love life and, curiously, they love death too! Fear of death vanishes and dying is understood to be a great experience.

With regard to freedom of consciousness, we take note of what Krishna says in the Gita:

As a person puts on new clothes, giving up old ones, the soul similarly accepts new material bodies, giving up the old and useless ones.

The soul can never be cut by any weapon, nor burnt by fire, nor moistened by water, nor withered by wind.
This individual soul is unbreakable, insoluble and can be neither burned nor dried. He is everlasting, present everywhere, unchangeable, immovable and eternally the same.

From the first verse above, it is clear that consciousness, which is an aspect of the soul, can free itself from the body. Radical Transformation of the mind takes one closer to the soul and engenders a release from the ego. That is why it is associated with what we termed earlier as the Radial Dive towards the Inner Being. Here, we are reminded of Jesus' statement, "The Kingdom of Heaven is within you." We can also see that the peace resulting from Radical Transformation is from the wider consciousness and not from the conditioned mind. In that sense, it can be said to pass all understanding through mental concepts. Experiencing Satori, when consciousness steps out of the body, is a state in which Radical Transformation is complete. Its beauty and profundity are clearly brought up by the narration of those who experience Satori.

The Emanation of the 'I'

During the inwardly directed attention, one can see that the 'I' is a product of thought and that it has no intrinsic substantiality. It is the assumption of that substantiality that causes problems. J. Krishnamurti's oft repeated statement, "The thinker is the thought," is relevant here. Self-awareness can take us to the breeding ground in the mind from where the 'I' emanates. That watchfulness prevents the 'I' from getting up and performing its usual dance, a dance that leads to much trouble to oneself and others. True Self can be discovered only when the 'I,' the false self, is no longer masquerading as the real one. In the absence of the 'I,' universality is felt in all happenings of our life. Naturally, such a perception brings about compassion towards everyone and everything.

The Chakras

Ancient sages of India have identified seven places in the human body as Spiritual Centers. These are known as 'Chakras,' They are so named because some kind of energy revolves like a wheel at those centers. 'Chakra' is the word for wheel in Sanskrit. When we are children, these Chakras maintain their rotation at a healthy speed. As we grow in age and let thought dominate our waking consciousness, they slow down leading to unhealthy physiology and proneness to disease. With awareness setting in, they begin to regain their original momentum and the body improves in health. It is known that these Chakras can be identified as the seven endocrine glands in our body. One of these glands, the

Thymus, usually becomes dormant at puberty. A strange thing is that it becomes reactivated and comes into action again in people whose self-awareness reaches some depth. Called the Heart Center, Ramana Maharishi and Aurobindo Ghose refer to it. Those who have entered the Esoteric Field can sense a pinprick type sensation in the region slightly to the right of the breastbone, the position of Thymus. The same sensation may also be felt at the Head Center (the Pineal gland). Generally, a person in the Esoteric Field comes to feel these two Chakras as a sort of early response of the human physiological system to growing awareness. It is said that thought permeates all cells of the body except the regions of the endocrine glands. Beginning from those clean regions, self-awareness starts clearing the thought residues from the other cells of the body.

Nadha Yoga

One of the things that help us free ourselves from the tyranny of thought is the willingness to direct our attention to what is happening around us at any given moment. To bring this into focus, we can close our eyes and listen to the sounds coming from different directions. This is called Nadha Yoga. Here Nadha is the word for sound in Sanskrit, and Yoga stands for the state of attention. It is a good feeling when we allow the sound waves to enter and vibrate within us. We may even get the feeling that they enter us not only through our ears but through the top of our head! Those who are familiar with the seven Chakras in our physical system may feel that sound enters through the Head Center. In any case, Nadha Yoga brings in some freedom from being occupied by thought. There is no need to set apart any routine practice time for this yoga. It is good to let it take place spontaneously as and when one is reminded of it by an inner call. Eckhart Tolle (Tolle, 2003) says that any disturbing noise can be as helpful as silence when we drop our resistance to the noise. During Nadha Yoga, we notice that a base of silence supports the vibrations of sound. Soon we sense that this silence is not the opposite of sound and that it has a cosmic content to it. Radical Transformation can have its beginnings and sustenance in the sensing of that silence.

Sounds around us can be of different kinds: Birds chirping, human voice from the next room or from across a field, rustle of leaves, music from a distance, the groaning whistle of a departing train, patter of rain on the roof, the murmur of distant thunder, cry of a baby and the swearing of a person whose car doesn't start!

In the night, Nadha Yoga takes on even more of a penetrative characteristic. Can we look at the face of a sleeping person in a sustained way? One senses deep serenity in that calm face and in the peaceful breathing. On such occasions, one's ego does not surface because the sleeping person's ego is not operative. Compassion surges up in us and, if we had said something hurtful to that person during the day, we resolve to apologize the next morning.

If we can let the serenity of the night keep us company during the day, life will be wonderful. It augments Radical Transformation. Further, it helps us deal with problems in relationships in a broad-minded way. We note here the statement made by the Divine Voice in *Conversations with God* (Walsch, 1995).

The Voice says that we cannot see the purpose behind relationships when we lose sight of each other as sacred souls on a sacred journey.

'No Challenge' as a Challenge!

On October 29, 2005, the *Democrat & Chronicle*, a newspaper of Rochester, NY, published an article with the headline, "Breast cancer survivor shares encouragement." A resident of Rochester was diagnosed of breast cancer in 1998. She thought she would die. However, after eight hours of surgery and eight months of chemotherapy, she recovered and "is now sitting happy, energetic, fit and grateful at the back of a store where she works part time." This news item quotes her as saying, "The little things in life that are taken for granted mean so much to me now. It is just a gift, a tremendous gift." The pointer here is that when people go through a shock, they are able to see things in better perspective and also sense the intrinsic beauty in the ordinary things of life. In other words, we wake up if we are confronted by a challenge. Each shock in our life is a challenge, minor or major. Now, the question here is: Can we wake up without the need for a shock? Reflection on this makes us appreciate life better. We understand the immaturity behind wallowing in self-pity and getting caught in the quagmire of self-centered activities. Inevitably, it increases our compassion towards people with whom we interact, our co-passengers on life's journey.

When life senses that we are already applying ourselves to appreciate its intrinsic beauty, it sees no need to wake us up with a shock. Life's tidings become calm helping us appreciate our proximity to Divinity and the beauty of life's journey. One might ask: What happens to one's karma in the event of such appreciation of life by us? The karmic momentum decreases as one's awareness increases. A mathematician would say they are inversely proportional; that is as one increases, the other decreases. If we can see beauty in the journey of life per se, self-awareness has gone to such an extent that karmic momentum becomes supportive rather than seeing the need to wake us up with some kind of suffering.

People who sense the meaning of the above two paragraphs might say, "Waking up under no challenge is the new challenge!"

The Esoteric Questions

Questions that do not have fixed answers through the intellect, and whose answers are experiential and not verbal, may be called Esoteric Questions. They are answered by sustained contact with them through Direct Awareness. Only those who find the questions to be sort of intriguing puzzles can maintain the interest in them. Answers to esoteric questions are living truths and cannot be contained in words. Like the light of dawn, they flower slowly from inside into the outer consciousness and progressively increase in intensity.

Who am I? Ramana Maharishi exhorts us to dwell on this question to discover the nature of the True Self. After some period of reflection, this question may undergo metamorphosis: from "Who am I?" to "Who is this I?" and then on to "How does this I emanate?" Such transformations of the question depend on individual psychology and that is what makes the process interesting. This question moves us on to the Radial Dive.

In this connection, we are guided by statements from esoteric writings such as the Upanishads and statements from Jesus Christ. In the Brihadaranyaka Upanishad, four Mahavakyas (Great Sayings) are given. One of them says, "Aham Brahmasmi," meaning, "One's True Self is the Divine Essence." It is reported (Mitchell, 1943) that someone asked Jesus Christ, "When will the Kingdom of God come?" And Jesus said, "The Kingdom of God will not come if you are looking for it. No one can say, 'It is here' or 'It is there,' for the Kingdom of God is within you." That gives us a hint on which way to go, the movement towards the Inner Self.

Is the world an illusion? We hear from the Masters that what the mind construes through its intellect from the report of the five senses is a kind of phantasmagoria, a kaleidoscopic view that makes things appear real while they are no more than mere mental projections. The rationalist's tools of judgment are within that phantasmagoria. His judgments would not be of much value because it would be like judging a dream from inside a dream. What kind of veracity can there be in such assessments? Nevertheless, those of us who have not gone to the 'other side' cannot mimic the Masters and repeat, like a parrot, that the world is an illusion. For example, when we have a toothache, it is very real; we don't say it is an illusion and continue to attend work that day. In fact, the toothache comes in as a valid excuse for our leave application! Its truth is so well acknowledged that our boss won't have any hesitation in sanctioning the leave. It is certainly not an illusion.

Does it mean that our Masters are wrong? Our judging the Masters would be like an elementary schoolchild from a nondescript village evaluating a Stanford University PhD thesis! So, on the one hand the world looks real to us but, on the other, the Masters say it is an illusion. Isn't it an interesting contradiction? It is not only the Masters but also those with a Satori experience who confirm the truth of this illusion.

While describing his Satori, one of them says: "It was Creation pure and simple and the things produced by the mind or the hand were at the outer fringes of this Creation with little significance." (Appendix 1) Another one under similar circumstances says, "The world of pain, suffering and sorrow was there and yet it was not." (Appendix 2)

The writer had an occasion to stay in an old building set in the forlorn ambience of village outskirts. It had a spooky look about it and you could have used that building for filming a thriller movie. Nonetheless, it had big windows and a generous stream of breeze through them. On one of the walls there was a mirror, about one foot square in size, with a small ledge at its base. While the writer was arranging his things in that building, a sparrow, presumably a male, flew in and settled down on the ledge of the mirror. The bird saw its own image and started pecking at it. Apparently, it was under the impression that there was a rival to it in the building. As one can easily sense, it could not drive the image-bird away. It was pecking vigorously and, of course, its rival was returning the pecks with equal vigor! A strange thing is that while the rival bird was illusory, its return blows were not! The poor bird was hurting its own beak. But it wouldn't give up easily. One could see that it was very concerned. We would like to make it clear to the sparrow that the other bird is only an illusion. But can we? That is perhaps the position of the Masters with regard to the rest of us when they talk about the world being an illusion.

Stark reality of the world has to be accepted as long as we are functioning in partial awareness and things are judged by the conditioned mind. When the cataclysmic change takes place due to deepening awareness, and our sensing center moves into the cosmic realm, certain 'Knowingness' takes place. Then, the truth of what the Masters say can be clear to us as a matter of firsthand experience.

A similar issue is the timelessness spoken of by the Masters. People who experience OBE and NDE have brief glimpses of that fact. For the ordinary people, however, that the world and time are illusions can only be hypotheses. Truth or falsehood of such hypotheses cannot be verified through the mere intellectual analysis. It needs clarity of non-verbal perception through Radical Transformation and the associated Direct Awareness. When ordinary people pass judgment on the statements of the Masters, they are unaware of a simple question: If the state of Enlightenment can be imagined from an unenlightened state, what difference can there be between the two?

Intriguing Questions: The following two questions can be puzzling:

1. Can one be in a state of meditation in which the 'meditator' is absent?

2. Can one be in a state of surrendering in which the 'surrenderer' is absent?

These questions won't make much sense to the conventional mind. For the esoterically inclined people, however, the same questions can open a door into the deeper consciousness. They would understand the state in which the ego does not interfere. Due to repeated inward attention, one sees how the waking consciousness can quietly release itself from the tyranny of the thought-ridden mind.

Questions from Taoism: The *Tao Te Ching* of Lao Tzu from China is well known for its esoteric view of life on this planet. It has appeared in English translation through different publications. Lao Tzu lived in China around the time of Buddha in India, about BCE 600. Much of what is written by him cannot appeal to the merely rational mind. However, there is a great deal for reflection in the inwardly turned enthusiasts. Just a few lines there can set us thinking for years after they are read. What we are interested in here are the questions raised in Poem 10 of that book. The following is the essence of those questions. It is good to investigate along these pointers as part of our inward awareness.

Can you go beyond the thought-ridden mind, hold to the One and never depart from it?

Can you pay attention to your breath and bring it down to the mellow state of a baby's breathing?

Can you cleanse your esoteric vision and wipe it until it is spotless?

Can you be like the female and allow passivity to open and shut heaven's gates?

Can you love all beings and govern them without being known?

Can you be aware of the four corners of the Earth and not interfere with them?

Reflections on these can help one discover the beauty of the deeper consciousness in us. As you take the inner dive into yourself to answer the esoteric questions, you find a wholesome response to life settling in you. Then you would generate your own esoteric questions!

Chapter 9

Death and the Message from NDE

One of the important issues to be considered in terms of the deeper understanding of life is its counterpart, namely, death. Many consider death as a morbid topic and avoid any discussion of it or at least show no interest in it. One of the reasons for the fear of death is the stark finality about it. The 'I' created by thought is accustomed to continuity, and so it is unable to sense what would happen if that continuity were cut. It is this uncertainty that comes up as fear of death. Turning away from the uncertainty is a kind of resistance to it and such refusal to look at it pushes the fear into the subconscious layers. From there it keeps sending messages through dreams and through loneliness during waking hours. This leads to looking for psychological attachments as these attachments give the 'I' a semblance of being secure. As a consequence, it creates images of others, gaining some comfort through the continuity sustained by the interaction with those images. Thus, a false base is created to feel safe and the fear of death is pushed under the carpet. However, somewhere in the deeper region, one knows that such comfort is false and so it prevents one from living fully. As we can see here, not paying attention to death affects life in the sense that its quality goes down. Living and dying are inextricably woven together and in their separation is the emergence of fear. We hear from the Masters that Truth has no continuity and that it is new from moment to moment. That is, there is a constant dying and renewal. Paying attention to death, one can move towards discovering that Truth because we can then see unity in the life-death pair. In other words, attention to the content of death helps us appreciate life better. Incidentally, it also aids the Radial Dive into oneself.

In his book *Stillness Speaks* (Tolle, 2003), Eckhart Tolle has a chapter titled "Death and the Eternal." His fluent presentation dwells on many esoteric items related to death. He says, "When death is denied, life loses its depth. The possibility of knowing who we are beyond name and form, the dimension of the transcendent, disappears from our lives because death is the opening into that dimension."

Other Masters have echoed the same in a simpler form: If you are afraid of death, you would be afraid of life.

In order to move on an exploratory journey into the topic of death, one has to set aside all preconceived notions and beliefs and come to it afresh. Therefore, consider all things you come across in this chapter as hypotheses to be verified in the light of your own awareness and curiosity to find out what lies in the dark. They are meant to kindle your eagerness for exploration rather than give fixity to concepts. After all, the phenomenon of death is around us during our lifetime and it is going to be at the end of our own. When we pay attention to the content of death, we begin to unravel its mystery, at least to some extent. There is a boldness that builds up with the understanding of the content and so the fear associated with death begins to dissolve. Two important consequences to this are:

1. We start treating people with deeper respect and compassion because we become focused on the fact that they may pass away at any time. One may ask: The transitory existence of people being well known, what contribution can there be from a study of death in enhancing one's compassion for people? Exploring into the region of death makes us befriend that phenomenon and so one can link it with one's people without fear and look at them from that perspective. Otherwise, associating people with death is so frightening that we cannot brook to see them in that light. Since death is understood to

be only a transition and not a final end, awareness of people's ongoing process after death makes us see them in an expansive and meaningful vista. We respect people as those who are here in their own right as evolving souls and not as those merely meant to satisfy our egoistic needs here. We see ourselves not held captive by the claustrophobia in time as if hedged in and contained by the duration between birth and death. That people are on a long journey and that we may meet them again makes us look at them with tenderness. These perspectives are not available to those who turn away from the study of death.

2. The boldness that builds up from applying ourselves to the study of death encourages us to delve more deeply into this intriguing field. We discover wonders from many recorded experiences, ancient and modern. 'Let me not turn towards that unpleasant thing' kind of resistance evaporates. The boldness fills our lives with a vibrancy that helps us lead a cheerful life and lift others also from their depression.

Mirthfulness resulting from an understanding of the after-death realm is indeed a rewarding feature. Not all after-death episodes are comforting. It means that the study does not merely build selfish hopes. It makes us responsible for how we are living our life here and now. That would help us tread the mysterious grounds in the afterlife with reassurance.

Unfortunately, many religious practices have only used the subject of death to coerce people into conformity through fear of punishment and hope of reward. This exploitation of people's fear of death in order to manipulate them into submission is a matter of poor conduct, to say the least. This is true of all exploitations of man's psychological weaknesses. Pushing more and more people into that type of religious conditioning can only serve to reduce the quality of man's consciousness on this planet. The sectarian approach to religion sustains the division among human beings and thus causes tension, violence and war in the world. Consequently, the evolution of consciousness on our Earth is effectively retarded.

Some religions, however, have talked about reincarnation, eliminating the claustrophobia in time, and hence the finality of death. This, no doubt, makes a difference. However, they have only marginally encouraged people to take up an impartial study of death and the afterlife as venerable topics.

Quite often, frightening stories of after-death periods have haunted people. It is a pity that such a fine topic as death and its aftermath is subjected to that kind of mistreatment. This is where research on near death experiences and reincarnation in recent years have contributed a great deal towards urging people to look into the beauty of what transpires after bodily death. It is good to alleviate people's fear of death through compassionate encouragement towards understanding the essence of death and the ongoing process.

Life and death are integral parts of a cyclic process in the form of creation, sustenance and dissolution, followed by creation again. A cyclic process alone can be eternal. The noisy mind can only think of a specific beginning and a specific ending because it functions on one directional movement of time. Many problems arise in the journey of life on account of the mind being tethered to this idea of static beginning (as one's birth) and static ending (such as an eternal heaven or eternal hell). Once we see beauty in the cyclic cosmological process, we are willing to happily participate in that Divine drama. Self-importance begins to dissolve and so working for personal salvation also goes out. This can help us bring in detachment because we understand that the cyclic movement is not towards any final destination. Thus, Enlightenment is in the Now and not at the end of a process. It comes through the understanding and realization of the cyclic process in the Now. Problems due to unidirectional time and the associated claustrophobia begin to vanish. This is not in the interest of the ego because a cyclic process eliminates the possibility of a predetermined, self-satisfying end, such as an eternal heaven. The ego refuses to acknowledge a fundamental law of the Universe: All that have a beginning will have an ending. Thus, if entering heaven signifies a beginning of a phenomenon, that phenomenon will have an ending too.

The Uneasy Event

There are two aspects of death to be looked into: The death of oneself and the death of another. The general psychological reactions to these two are somewhat different but understanding death as a general process brings on a unifying response to both these aspects of death.

A number of factors deserve exploration. Death of a relative or a friend causes a strangely negative feeling. It is hard to put one's finger on it when it comes to naming that feeling. In general, it is described as sadness. But it is in fact a combination of feelings. At least, the following three are involved:

1. Guilty feeling for not having been kind to the person when the person was around.
2. That person himself or herself did not have a happy life.
3. Cavity made in one's consciousness by that person's absence, the associated loneliness and self-pity.

The first one can be mostly eliminated by understanding the value of compassion and gentle behavior. This is where being aware of the Mental Content in each one that responds to situations can be helpful, as mentioned in chapter 7. In general, entering the Esoteric Field brings in a natural state of empathy and compassion. Empathy, meaning the ability to understand what the other is going through, is one field where the human being can show greater ability than the animal. In some other areas, however, animals may show better psychology!

About the second item given above, something can be done if we are alert enough to care for the person while the person is alive. However, a lot depends on that person's ability to lead a happy life and not much can be done by others. Here, however, one's knowledge of the after-death process through near death experiences (NDEs) can help one free oneself from the sadness because of the insight gained on the afterlife.

The third one is indeed a helpful occurrence that can make one be pensive and bring about deepening awareness. To some extent, understanding reincarnation and the long journey on the cyclic process helps us meet this challenge in a healthy way. This is true with regard to the thought of one's own death too.

Thought breeds fear, as J. Krishnamurti would often say. It is the Radial Dive and the associated inner transformation that can free us from the tyranny of thought. The inwardly directed movement takes us Home! That is the Home from which we came and so entering it is not a new beginning.

We now explore questions that arise with regard to the phenomenon of death. Regardless of the way in which a given culture may treat it, the questions seem to be pretty much the same. In her book *Death: The Final Stage of Growth*, Elisabeth Kübler-Ross lists them in a comprehensive way (Kübler-Ross, 1975). The following is a modified summary of it.

What happens to us after we die? Is there a meaning to death? Is there a relationship between our life on Earth and the after-death period? Is there a continuity of some form after death? What is its nature? Are there ways in this life that will better prepare us for death or for an afterlife? Is there any meaning to human existence and can understanding death help us lead a peaceful life? What is gained by paying attention to the afterlife? Will we come back to this Earth for another life, many lives? If so, does this depend on how we lived our previous lives? Or are we destined at death only to disintegrate and let the body become absorbed by the Earth?

When we playfully enter the investigation posed by the above questions and sustain the interest for a while, we begin to enjoy it. Given that we are not tethered to any belief or disbelief, the movement in freedom becomes a journey of discovery. The associated understanding is what frees us from the fear of death. Any freedom from fear that comes from a belief becomes shaky when that belief is confronted by another belief or disbelief. As J. Krishnamurti puts it, the peacefulness that comes through beliefs is like the leaf which appears to be calm but begins to flutter with the next breeze. Peace resulting from non-verbal understanding, through Direct Awareness, is irreversible and so unshakable.

It is said that the Buddha encouraged his disciples to visit the morgue or cremation ground frequently, to be among the dead bodies. The associated non-verbal understanding can go a long way.

The Psychological Death: The word death is usually associated with the ending of the body. It is a break in continuity. Continuity is provided by the mind, by thought. The essence of that continuity is through a form, the form provided by the body. Thought feeds on it. When the continuity is threatened, thought comes up with fear. So, fear is a result of the habitual neurology and not something that can exist by itself. In other words, it has no intrinsic substantiality. When this process is seen through deepening awareness, something takes place in the hidden region of our minds. Continuity provided by thought begins to dissolve. This dissolution of continuity is psychological death. Masters say that there is then living from moment to moment. The thought process needed to run an efficient practical life will, however, continue; only there is no continuing 'I,' the image, that is afraid of death.

Eckhart Tolle has an interesting statement to make regarding the secret of life (Tolle, 2001). He says that if one 'dies' before one actually dies, one realizes that there is no death. The first 'dies' refers to the psychological death and the second one to the bodily demise. When psychological death takes place, we become one with the essence that is imperishable and so there is no more the possibility of death. Bodily death is seen only as a change in form. These concepts are easier said than perceived but, certainly, they do work to improve our clarity.

The Mini Death Experience

There are occasions when a human being comes close to death and actually crosses the border between life and death for a short period. However, they return to normal life following a ravishing experience during the period when they are considered clinically dead. This phenomenon may be called a Mini Death Experience. However, the pioneers in this field have preferred to call it a Near Death Experience (NDE). So, we follow suit.

Elisabeth Kübler-Ross and Raymond Moody did much research work on near death experiences (Kübler-Ross, 1969, 1975; Moody, 1975, 1988). Later, several other researchers were drawn into investigating this esoteric experience. They have collected a lot of information and have analyzed it intelligently over the past fifty years or so to provide us with interesting perspectives. Some years ago, if one had an NDE, that person was reluctant to talk about it for fear of being called 'crazy'; they may be admitted to an asylum! But now there is growing awareness among people about the intrinsic profundity of that experience. It may take some more decades before it becomes the common man's knowledge. Your present interest in it is a contributory factor towards that end. Those who apply themselves to this subject in a dedicated way are sure to bring about a transformation in their psychology that will enrich their lives as well as the lives of their near and dear ones. It would augment in-depth peace of mind. That, in turn, will help the evolution of collective consciousness on this planet.

A near death experience usually takes place under severe conditions of physical suffering, such as due to an accident, serious illness or heart attack. Quite often, the NDE occurs when the patient is undergoing an operation for revival. It coincides in time with the period when both the cardiac and the cerebral signals of the person are flat indicating that the patient is clinically dead. The period lasts for about five to ten minutes in most cases but sometimes it is longer. When they are inside the experience, however, the time sense seems to be totally different. Frequently, they experience the past, present and future all at the same time with the result that the conventional reckoning of time has no relevance to it. It is interesting to note that those who undergo the Satori experience (Advaita), as mentioned in chapter 4, also talk about similar timelessness. When we see that Satori is a result of inner transformation, and has nothing to do with any bodily suffering, this fact of similarity in the sensing of time gives additional credibility to the NDE as a spiritual experience. It looks like this parallel is not yet looked into in the research on NDE.

The following is an attempt at presenting a summary of current understanding on near death experiences. It is by no means exhaustive and should be considered as a brief attempt at presenting the salient features of that dimension of consciousness.

Near death experiences come up with many significant characteristics; not all of them occur in every NDE. Why is this so? Research is still at a nascent stage with regard to answering this and many other questions. Maybe we will know the answers only on the other side! It can, however, be safely said that each characteristic is experienced by several people and a few people experience all of them. They are enumerated below:

1. Starts with an out-of-body awareness. (Peacefulness and total relief from pain.)
2. The Tunnel experience
3. Meeting deceased relatives or friends
4. The Light and its embrace
5. Life review
6. Extraordinary settings
7. "Do you want to come this way or go back?"
8. Reentry into the body; feeling the pain

The first significant change noticed during an NDE is the release of consciousness from the body, generally known as an out-of-body experience (OBE). It was briefly mentioned in chapter 8. Like a centered spirit, one's consciousness leaves the body and hovers near the roof, if they happen to be in a room at that time. We will call it the 'Entity' for our description. The Entity sees one's own body lying on the operating table with physicians and nurses working on it. After the NDE is over, the patient is able to accurately describe what was going on (including such minor issues as which nurse slipped and fell!), much to the amazement of everyone because the patient had no pulse and was considered stone-dead at that time. Presumably, the patient's eyes were closed with a cloth, and, even if they were open, the brain could not have recorded anything. Frequently, the Entity moves out of the room and goes around, even recognizes one's relatives and friends in the waiting room, as corroborated by the Entity's later narration. That baffles all.

When the Entity tries to communicate during the OBE, nobody seems to be aware of its presence and movement. If the Entity touches someone for attention, his hand goes right through the body of that someone, as if that person is made of gas! That is when the Entity begins to notice that oneself is dead, gone! His earthly being is out. The touch of finality that sensing gives can be very sad. The impossibility of the usual communication (and the irreversibility of it) is what delivers the deeply sorrowful state.

Around that occurrence, the Entity begins to move through a tunnel (or some characteristic passage) at a considerable speed. The tunnel is dark; you have never seen anything that dark in your earthly life. The movement is towards a light at the end of the tunnel. During this movement, the Entity may meet a relative or friend who had already passed away. That person appears fresh and younger than last seen, while also being imbued with genuine love and affection. It is made clear that the receiver is there to ease the transition of the Entity into the new realm, the discarnate world. Sometimes, the receiver may say it is not yet time for the Entity to be there and, in such cases, there may be a sudden return to the body. In most cases, however, the movement towards the light continues until the Entity lands in the bosom of the light, a light with supreme brilliancy that does not hurt the eye. Again, you have never seen anything like that in your earthly life. From here onwards it would only seem appropriate to use the capital 'L' for the light. The Light then speaks to the Entity in direct communication and not through successive words as done on the Earth. The Entity is flooded with infinite compassion from the Light. (After returning to the body, the person usually says with conviction that the Light is no other than God or Divinity, as one may put it.)

While being bathed in this Light and its compassion, the Entity is usually shown a review of the events in the life just completed on the Earth. Some people have said that it is like a movie while others talk about a three-dimensional display of all events: Past, present and future. While going through the review, stops are made to pay attention to such items where compassionate alternative behavior is pointed out. The review spells out the sad or happy state of mind of those who received the action from the Entity while on the Earth. It seems like an education for wholesome behavior in future lives. The most significant aspect of this review is that the Entity is never made to feel guilty for some unkind behavior or acts of impropriety on one's part. No idea of punishment is ever indicated or implied. This underlines the simple fact that in the Divine field of compassion there can be no room for any punishment or 'Get it back now' kind of scenario.

Many Masters, including Jesus Christ, have emphatically said, "God is love," instead of saying, "God loves us." The profundity of their statement comes from the fact that if God can love, He can also hate, but if God *is* love, there can be no hate from Him. It is significant that people who go through NDE have a firsthand experience of what the Masters implied.

We now continue with the NDE sequence of events. At the end of the review, the Entity faces a question from the Light: Do you want to stay or go back? Even though the atmosphere is wonderful in the presence of the Light and one would like to remain in that beatific world, the Entity quite often decides to come back to the earthly life because that person feels a left-over responsibility. One's aging parents or some young children need the presence of the Entity down here. The same feeling may be there because of some unfinished work too. The moment such a feeling occurs, the Entity is immediately back in the body. There is a feeling of frustration in leaving the wonderful atmosphere of the other side. Concurrently, physical pain in the body returns.

There are cases where the Entity is allowed to visit some extraordinary region that would fit our description of a heaven. In that case, the above question occurs after the visit to that 'heaven.' Many ramifications of the above features occur, making the study of NDE quite intriguing.

What makes NDE a valuable experience is that it lets us imbibe a wider perspective about life and death; further, it opens a vista of holistic application leading to wholesome living. The incomparable Divine compassion in which one is bathed during NDE, no matter how small its duration, seems to be the key factor in giving great depth and beauty to that experience. It is clear, from the responses of both children and adults who have had NDE, that the experience has the touch of a catharsis. The person is never the same on the lee side of the NDE. No experience due to a drug or hallucination ever remains in memory that long, nor do they bring about a Radical Transformation in the person towards a 'dharmic' life.

Traumatic experiences do leave a trail but only for a while, maybe for some years, and then gradually wear out, but that due to an NDE remains with the same intensity till the person's last day, and perhaps even afterwards! Further, traumas engender an unpleasant disposition while an NDE does exactly the opposite.

Absence of guilt and punishment during the NDE is what makes it a wholesome experience with a touch of the Divine. If it had been triggered by conventional religious or cultural conditioning, it could not have this scenario during the review. Such conditioning is a result of corruption by man's thought. It has been found that NDEs are not affected by nationality, religion and the like. A few cases do show cultural influence at the times of interpretation and not at the time of experiencing. It is the universality of this experience that gives the NDE its much-deserved respect. Anything related to fundamental truth has this characteristic of universality. Take for example the simple fact of Earth's gravity. It is not one thing for the American and another for the Egyptian, and so on. Anything that lacks universality, as a result of man-made divisions and sectarian influence, cannot hold truth. The Esoteric Field is universal in all the things that it puts forth.

Camaraderie and bonhomie are two wonderful things in our lives that lead to in-depth harmony and a peaceful life. Those who go through NDE find these a natural part of their psychology after the experience. Zest for life increases and fear of death disappears. Empathy reaches a high level and there is an eagerness to have knowledge about variegated Divine manifestations on the Earth.

Not all of us can have an NDE but, just reflecting on the statements of those who have had the experience, we can understand certain esoteric truths and reap the benefits. It is an ocean and drinking even a drop from it can perform wonders.

Those who feel drawn by an inner call to the Esoteric Field will find NDE an exciting and stimulating subject. Among many good books in this field, *The Light Beyond* by Raymond Moody is an excellent one (Moody, 1988). Dr. Moody produces effective counterpoints to a number of skeptical criticisms on NDE. The book titled *The Complete Idiot's Guide to Near Death Experiences* has exhaustive coverage of the paranormal phenomenon (Atwater and Morgan, 2005). (After one starts reading a few pages in that book, one may feel that the word *Idiot's* may have to be removed from the title!) In it, the topic of NDE is observed from different angles including those of the skeptics. In *Transformed by the Light*, Dr. Melvin Morse investigates children's NDEs (Morse, 1992). A particularly interesting article on NDE, "I Died at 10:52 AM" by Victor Solow, was published in *Reader's Digest* (Solow, 1974). He talks about the extraordinary silence on the other side and the feeling of being part of a harmonious whole.

The Truth of Reincarnation

Man-made systems can only succeed in pushing fear of death into the subconscious regions and not help to face it objectively. This is because such systems sustain the ego as evidenced by the emotional attachment to the systems. Mere hope of reward can only serve as an escape and cannot lead to understanding the phenomenon of death. Further, all this is clothed over by some comforting beliefs and thus fear recedes to the background and hides there. These facts, though obvious to the impartial observer, can be disturbing to some religious people. That very thing shows their peace to be a shaky one. A shakable peace is no peace at all; it is a deception. The same thing is true of reincarnation. If it comes in merely as a belief, it does not have much value. Understanding reincarnation is a different matter from holding on to a belief about it, just as it is with the topic of death. What is needed is an eagerness to understand the truth and not get carried away by conformity to beliefs or disbeliefs, no matter how comforting they may be. The peace that comes through understanding death as part of a unitary process (and not as an ending) is imbued with an in-depth serenity and is not shakable at all.

In order to test the validity of some subjective or intangible issue, such as NDE or reincarnation, an approach called the MEMP analysis can be helpful. As briefly mentioned in chapter 7, MEMP stands for Mutually Exclusive Multiple Pointers. In that approach, we sense the intrinsic validity of something when several unconnected issues point to the same thing, as shown in the following representation.

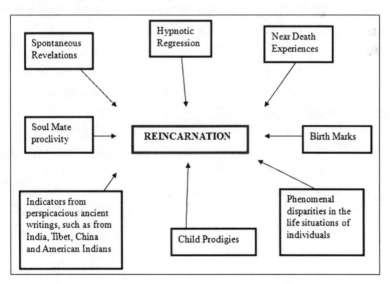

Fig. 9 The Pointers for the Truth of Reincarnation

We see that the theme of reincarnation is supported by at least eight mutually exclusive pointers. The following paragraphs give a brief explanation of these eight supporting features.

Pointer 1. Spontaneous Revelation: A number of human beings from all cultures have had spontaneous surges of past life memories, the person being thrown unexpectedly into it. Research on reincarnation has collected a great deal of information on this. What is noteworthy is that a large number of individuals reported in those investigations are from cultures that deny reincarnation. An interesting case is that of General Patton of the US Army who served in the Second World War. His experience is given below.

After the war was over, General Patton was traveling in a car with his friends at a place in Italy. While they were moving along the countryside with groves, Patton became very pensive, kept looking out of the window and stopped talking to his friends. They noticed the change in him. At one point he asked for the car to be stopped, opened the door and started walking away towards a plain with some trees. He was gone for a while and then returned walking slowly back to the car. His eyes were filled with tears. The bemused friends waited for an explanation. After he collected himself, Patton expressed his feelings. The essence of his communication could be phrased as follows:

> From the time we moved into the countryside, there was a strong feeling that I was here before. The feeling was intense and so I told our friend to stop the car and took a walk. After I had walked some distance, the scene began to change. There were Roman soldiers moving around in the plains involved in a war and I was one of them. It was such a vivid scene that I could clearly perceive even the details. It went on for a while and then began to fade until I found myself back in the

present. When I came out of the vision, it was more than clear to me that what transpired was a past life experience of mine.

Patton, along with many other members of his family, often claimed to have seen vivid, lifelike visions of their ancestors. He saw truth in reincarnation, and much anecdotal evidence indicates that he held himself to be the reincarnation of the Carthaginian general Hannibal, a Roman legionnaire, a Napoleonic field marshal, and various other past military figures. Some details of these are given in Wikipedia, the free encyclopedia on the Internet.

Skeptics are likely to reject General Patton's experience as nothing but a mere hallucination. We would agree with them if General Patton's was the only one of its kind, an isolated experience. In reality, though, researchers have collected a fund of information on such Spontaneous Revelations over the last thirty years. In this connection, interested readers will find the book *Lifetimes* by Frederick Lenz a fascinating book to read (Lenz, 1979). In it, Frederick gives several interesting accounts of Spontaneous Revelations narrated by his correspondents in America. One particular study in it, among others, is so amazing that it seems to establish reincarnation as an undeniable fact. It is one of the veridical cases, cases which give the opportunity to verify the accounts. The findings tallied accurately with the details given by the correspondent. In this case, Frederick himself did the verification exercise.

Some critics deny the validity of hypnotic regression based on their assumption that leading suggestions come from the hypnotist himself. Those critics will have a hard time defending their position when facing cases of Spontaneous Revelation.

Pointer 2. Hypnotic Regression: As the reader may already be aware, hypnotic regression implies going back in memory, touching the events of life through hypnosis. Over the last several decades, this method has been effectively used by therapists and others to cure people of ailments and phobias. When regressing, the person under hypnosis comes into contact psychologically with some happening that had been the source of the present problem. Such a contact is found to relieve the person of the problem almost immediately. Regressing may take the subject to a past event in this life or, as happens quite often, to some event in a past life. In her book *You Have Been Here Before* (Fiore, 1981), Dr. Edith Fiore describes several sessions of hypnotic regression with her subjects. She took them into their past lives and cured them of insomnia, sexual frigidity, chronic headaches, fear of heights and many other problems. The fact that contact with a past-life event almost always cures the person of a malady indicates that we carry residues from our past lives. As a matter of spiritual growth, the soul keeps track of them. Dr. Fiore says that in her work on reincarnation, she finds not even one aspect of character or human behavior that cannot be better understood through an examination of past-life events. Her patients moved hypnotically into previous existences to find the sources of their talents, skills, interests, strengths and weaknesses, as well as of happiness and suffering. Dr. Fiore feels that the tapestry of our lives is woven with threads that are ancient, making the pattern a complex one.

Pointer 3. Near Death Experiences: There are two pointers from NDEs, one indirect and the other direct, to establish authenticity of the fact that we live many lives. The indirect pointer is the Life Review item that quite a few people go through during an NDE. Here events of the life just lived come along like a movie for the person to feel the effects of one's actions on others. The compassionate Light seems to gently indicate kinder alternatives to handling those occasions where one had been unkind. The Entity is given a sort of lesson. Of what value is this review if everything is finished with the life just lived? Simple common sense would tell us that such a review has meaning only if the Entity has another life or more lives to live.

The following episode given by Jean Ritchie in her book *Death's Door* is a direct pointer to reincarnation (Ritchie, 1996).

Ms. Jean Allen had her NDE as a result of a horrific accident with a chain saw that she used to cut logs of wood for her fireplace. At the time of the mishap, the saw cut through her cheek, neck, chest and left arm. She was rushed to the hospital and a medical team spent three hours working on her, inserting many stitches. Before the medical work started, Ms. Allen had a two-hour wait and it was during this time that she had her NDE. She said that the NDE took away the fear of death and that it gave her a lot of faith in life.

The author of the book goes on to say that many people who experience NDE report a much greater sensitivity to the supernatural. Ms. Allen felt that she had become receptive to them since her NDE. Further, after the NDE, she was convinced that she had lived several previous lives. While she had quite clear memories of the recent two, her memories of the earlier ones were vague.

Vital Signs is a newsletter type periodical published by the International Association for Near-Death Studies (IANDS; iands. org). Amazing accounts of NDE are published in it frequently. In its Volume 25, Number 1, there is an article with the title "Death Before Dying: A Love Experience" contributed by Andy Petro (Petro, 2006). One would like to present the whole article here for the sheer beauty of its contents. Unfortunately, space does not permit it. However, an extract from it is given below.

In my Life Review, I was completely surrounded by my countless lives. I could feel, taste, smell, hear and view each experience and relive each and every event exactly as I remembered it in 'real life'. Everywhere I looked, there was another 'life experience' connected to another life experience, seamlessly presented through an invisible, undetectable connection. I knew that I was in what I now call the 'Eternal Now.'

Thus, after their NDE, quite a few people have reported having lived many lives and so NDE can be considered a good pointer towards the truth of reincarnation.

Pointer 4. Birth Marks: Trutz Hardo conducted research on children from several countries to verify the truth of reincarnation. In his book *Reincarnation* (Hardo, 2003), case histories of children who remembered their past lives are given. Those children are from England, Germany, the USA, Lebanon, South Africa, Israel, India, Brazil, Sri Lanka and Turkey. Scientists such as Dr. Ian Stevenson, Director of the Division of Personality Studies at the Health Sciences Center, University of Virginia, report on how the children's statements were put to test in order to check their validity.

Cases which are especially convincing are those in which the children are born with missing limbs. Those children are able to describe exactly where and when they lost their limbs in a past life. They also often know precisely who their parents and relatives where in that life and where they lived. When the children's statements were subjected to scientific verification, they invariably turned out to be true. What is interesting is that children who form the subjects of this study are from such widely varied cultures that mere cultural conditioning could not have caused them to talk about past lives. In fact, quite a few countries chosen in Trutz Hardo's study are those in which reincarnation as a theme is vehemently denied.

He says that there is an incredible number of birth defects for which the medical profession is unable to find a cause. He points out that Stevenson has clearly demonstrated through his investigations that one of the most influential causes leading to birth defects is the transfer of physical marks from a past life. In this regard, the story of Cemil Hayek of Turkey carrying bullet wounds from a past life is one of the most convincing cases, among many others, recorded in Hardo's book.

Pointer 5. Phenomenal Disparities in Life Situations: It is obvious that people's lives on this planet show tremendous variation, in terms of their physical and mental well-being, circumstances and opportunities. Some are born into royal families and some as beggars, some as beautiful and capable as to win a Miss World title, and others with blatant birth deformities and handicaps. There are people like Apollonius, the Greek, who could do advanced mathematics of that time as an early teenager and there are those now who cannot comprehend it even at the age of forty!

How can we explain such disparities if there is only one life? It would be an unfortunate and unfair condemnation of some to be so much on the negative side throughout their life, while they see their counterparts enjoying all the good things. "Why me?" would be an obvious question in their minds. People who deny reincarnation must consider this as an important issue.

On this, a plausible explanation can be offered by the theme of reincarnation. There are many variegated life conditions on this planet and the soul would like to participate in as many as possible in its journey towards the Supreme. It knows that the negative circumstance it is going through is meant to experience that side of life too. One understands that it is a passing thing; the soul would have other lives in which it can enjoy the brighter side. Both conditions, positive and negative, can help self-awareness to grow. As a result, one comes to know the True Self, leading to the final reunion with Divinity. Such awareness also helps us not to look down upon our less fortunate fellow beings as we too might have gone through those circumstances in a past life or may do so in a future one. Correspondingly, megalomania does not set in as a result of our own situation being glamorous.

This understanding builds our fortitude because we see that souls go through many circumstances through many lives and so all incidents have their own meaning in the total scheme of things. Thus, we do not wallow in self-pity. There is also the fact that this Earth has so much to offer that one life is too short a time to experience all its gifts. Perhaps there are other planets in the universe that offer even more and it would be a pity to pack up and leave after one life on Earth to some place of imagined gratification.

Pointer 6. Child Prodigies: Here we should briefly look at the work done by Edgar Cayce (Langley, 1967), known as the Sleeping Prophet. He lived in the first half of the twentieth century in the southern part of the USA. For about forty years of his life, he gave past-life readings to many people and those were archived as 'Life Readings,' numbering more than 14,000. Those brief speeches were given by Cayce under a state of self-hypnosis when he could peer through others' past-life occurrences. He made a stir in the West by revealing the truth that each person lives many lives on this planet. In later years, several researchers used his Life Readings to get an insight into the subject of reincarnation. One of them is Gina Cerminara who published her findings in a book with the title *Many Mansions* (Cerminara, 1950). If you are a person looking for deep meaning to life, you will find this book quite absorbing.

Cerminara's scholarly writing brings forth the value of past-life studies. She observed the gradual spiritual and other developments of human beings over a span of several lifetimes. She says that acceptance of the reincarnation principle illumines as if by a floodlight the unknown background to many an issue in the current life. The landscape thus illumined is fascinating.

Its principal importance is that we can discern the slow winding paths over many lives in which capacities, traits and attitudes of the present are achieved. Cerminara adds that it is as if reincarnation revealed the submerged eight-ninth of an iceberg while psychologists have strained themselves to examine the exposed one-ninth.

The truth of the above is vindicated in several ways when we observe with insight the varied maturity and capabilities of human beings. This is especially striking with regard to child prodigies and geniuses. It is known that Mozart's musical genius was noticed as early as the age of three. His first compositions were written when he was only five years old. It is said that he could play the piano blindfolded at just six years of age; sometimes even with crossed hands! As simple common sense would tell us, such prodigious development of the human brain is unthinkable in the absence of long-standing input from several lives.

A recent example of the child prodigy in India is that of U. Srinivas who plays the South Indian classical music on the mandolin. He gave performances to elite audiences well before he reached his teens. It is known that the kind of music he performed is a difficult art and to be good at it needs a simultaneous sensing of several precise items by the human brain. Added to it is the fact that this music requires continuous transitional frequencies of notes, unlike most of those in the West which thrive on discrete frequencies. The mandolin is essentially a discrete frequency instrument, unlike the violin. It needs indeed an adept to be good at it under the demands of continuous frequencies of the music. Again, such genius is unthinkable unless there is a long history behind it in the individual's development over past lives. There have been many such prodigies in India and abroad throughout history, not only in the field of music but in other fields as well.

Pointer 7. Indicators from Perspicacious Ancient Writings: Some ancient cultures, such as those of India, Tibet, China and Native Americans, showed interest in understanding the hidden aspects of life, body and mind. They were more consumed by application to that avenue rather than to the development of material aspects of life. European culture, on the other hand, did a great deal to promote the latter and so came up with wonderful developments in science and technology. When we recognize this dichotomy, we can appreciate the two essential avenues available for human evolution in the interior and the exterior worlds respectively. The dichotomy is also observed in the circumferential and Radial Dive type perceptions mentioned in chapter 4. Cultures that respected the Radial Dive could obviously have deep insights into the hidden aspects of life. Such perspicacity arises as a result of intuition taking the lead over the merely rational mind.

In *Commentaries on Living* (Rajagopal, 1991), a Westerner meets J. Krishnamurti to discuss the place of knowledge in discovering the truth. He says that scientific and medical acumen, the basis for development of the material world, is rooted principally in the consciousness of the Western man, just as in the consciousness of the Eastern man there is the perceptive ability to fathom the otherworldliness. However, we observe that there have been some exceptions to this general rule either way.

"Unity in Diversity" was sensed very early by the sages of India and China. They each had a term for representing that Ultimate Essence: Brahman and Tao respectively. Thus, amidst the apparent chaos, they could perceive the hidden harmony and the One Truth that supports everything. Added to it was also the understanding of the connectedness of everything which led to sensing the fact that nothing happens by chance. With that kind of penetration, non-apparent issues like reincarnation could be intuitively understood. Given that scenario, it is easy to see that cultures of the East have a say on the recondite issues of life and death.

In the Bhagavad Gita, Krishna says, "Arjuna, you and I have lived many lives; while I remember them all, you have forgotten them."

Buddha's presentations had always a backdrop of karma and its consequences. There have been such assertions in the writings of other ancient cultures too.

Pointer 8. Soulmate Proclivity: During our lifetime we interact with many people: Relatives, friends, colleagues, acquaintances and even strangers! We notice that with some we strike harmony easily but with others it is fraught with difficulties. There are some with whom we become chummy without apparent reasons and with some there seems to be baseless antagonism right from the beginning. Further, with a few, we feel tremendously drawn towards them. There is then the soulmate feeling between the individuals. Because mere logic fails to explain these strange occurrences, such mental proclivities can be said to arise from past-life associations. Dr. Lenz has devoted a chapter in his book *Lifetimes* to the matter of soul-mate proclivity (Lenz, 1979). He says that in 28 cases of remembrances, people saw that they had been associated in several of their past lives with someone in the current life. When the two met in this life, they felt strongly drawn to each other without an apparent cause. They found that they were happy to be together irrespective of their stations and vocations in life. Sooner or later, either one or both of them had spontaneous revelations in which they saw that they had a similar intimacy in many of their previous lives.

Dr. Lenz's findings show that one can have more than one soulmate and that soulmates can be of either gender. As mentioned before, Dr. Lenz's subjects view past-life scenes in waking awareness and not under hypnosis. Understanding such influence of past lives helps us deal intelligently with current problems and blessings in personal relationships.

Thus, the eight pointers above clearly support the actuality of reincarnation. By the way, that paradigm also serves to bring out an example of MEMP application. People interested in exploring esoteric issues would find the MEMP approach meaningful and stimulating. What is not considered above is the possibility of negative pointers, those that point away from the central issue and so contradict the possibility. For example, with regard to reincarnation, people may ask: "If the same people are reborn, how does the population increase?" This pointer seems to discount reincarnation. An explorer must consider all possibilities. This particular question, however, is effectively answered by Edgar Cayce and others (Khoo, 2014) based on perceptions extended over the last ten thousand years. Its details are not reproduced here because they are beyond the scope of this book. Interested people are directed to the publications given under References at the end of the book. In the process of MEMP application, one's own intuition comes up at some stage and pronounces the truth or falsehood of the issue at hand. Thus, the real proof comes from inside one, a matter of inner perception and not one from a second person. Proofs advanced by another person can always be thwarted by the 'explaining away' attitude of a logical mind. In other words, either one knows through one's own direct inner sensing (due to the building up of perception from honest exploration) or the truth cannot be known merely through a proof given by another person.

In any investigation, one must be wary of both favorable and unfavorable prejudices interfering with the movement towards the Truth. We must keep in mind the adage, "One believes what one wants to believe." The deep feeling to discover the actuality coupled with a reliance on the inner awareness can prevent us from going astray.

Understanding the True Self

Investigation of death and the afterlife is helpful in understanding who we are beyond the thought-projected image of us; that is moving from the form to the formless. This understanding takes place as a growing intensity of self-awareness when there is no moving away from the 'Now.' The moving away causes one to hold on to unsubstantial things and so it sustains a troubled state of mind. Death reminds us of the insubstantiality of mind-projected things and thus can urge us to pay attention to that which lies beyond the transient. The ephemeral cannot be intrinsically substantial. Understanding life and death can help us move towards that which does not come and go. That is the key to knowing who we truly are.

If a very big circle is drawn, a small bit of its circumference looks like a straight line. Thus, when awareness is limited, there appears to be only the period between birth and death, and hence one life only. As awareness expands, one begins to sense the curved aspect of the line and the vast circle of which the bit is a part, a tiny part. Then one becomes aware of the cyclic process and hence of reincarnation. It is this expanding awareness that at some point helps us jump out of the circle, into the Immensity.

Manifestation of the universe and its contents are held in Universal Consciousness. This manifestation is what takes place in a cyclic process. Let us again visualize this process as a circle drawn on a sheet. Individual processes have their beginning and ending on this circle. For any given point, there are always points behind and points ahead. These represent the past and future of a given process. As long as a process belongs to the circle, which is to the manifestation, it will have a beginning and an ending. All items conceived by the mind, including heaven and the like, belong to this manifestation. What lies beyond the manifestation and, therefore, outside the circle has no beginning and no ending. Masters call it the Absolute. The circle is binding in the sense that as long as one is on it, laws of Prakriti (nature) apply and all things are connected; nothing happens by chance. When we talk of Enlightenment, it is a matter of freedom from the circle, a matter of jumping off from the circle, into the Absolute. Then Prakriti can no longer have its way. This freedom is Liberation. Through deepening awareness, the mind is freed from its projections and 'the jumping off' from the circle takes place. As long as we are on the circle (which is what happens when we identify ourselves as individuals), birth, death and reincarnation are facts, but outside the circle there is neither birth nor death, and so no reincarnation either. Our understanding of who we truly are makes us jump off the circle.

Some Masters alert us to the fact that reincarnation cannot help if, in the next incarnation, we still continue to be thought ridden as in the present; that will obstruct self-knowledge and we will continue to be ignorant of who we are. So, what is needed is attention to the esoteric aspects, here and now, that can help us understand ourselves; otherwise, the mind keeps us arrested on its egoistic projections: A pleasurable heaven after death, better life in the next incarnation and the like. Cosmological awareness is expansive and so is helpful in discovering who we truly are. It is good to know where we are in regard to the total scheme of things so that the present makes sense and we can pay loving attention to it. Ignorance of the movement of the soul in regard to the total journey, across many incarnate and discarnate periods, can lead to perversion; it would allow the mind with its limited perspective to rule the roost. So, it is awareness of reincarnation that helps us while dependence on it for change can be counterproductive.

Chapter 10

Good Health

It may appear a little out of the way for some to find a chapter on a down-to-earth topic such as physical health amidst topics dealing with deeper psychological aspects of life's journey. Others may feel that it would provide a refreshing change from continuously dealing with the noisy mind. Besides, attention to good health is not as difficult as it is to the inner transformation. So, this is a region where we can have a better grip on what is happening. Such pep items are always welcome.

In the previous chapters, we touched on several aspects of the human mind caught unconsciously for centuries in the habit of thought. The associated awareness helps one bring about a vibrant life, though not at the early stages of attention. Some adjustment period is involved. Once interest in the Esoteric Field takes over, it never withers; it only furthers itself in intensity. Very soon, awareness associated with that interest brings about a calmer and quieter mind in contrast to the state engendered by the habitual, unconscious living. While this attention to the mind is essential in bringing about the inner dive and the associated transformation, attention to the body is equally important. There is a Tamil proverb: *Suvarai Vaithukkonduthan chithiram ezhutha vendum*. It means that for producing a painting or a drawing, a good background, such as a wall or a board, is necessary. It is obvious that the body provides such a background on which evolution of consciousness can take place. Therefore, for bringing about the inner transformation in a person, good physical health is quite essential.

Aside from the above logical argument, the body, an amazing mechanism, deserves attention in its own right. Our physical outfit, a product of cosmological intelligence, is a fine example of Divine manifestation in terms of intricacies and coordination. If one listens to a medical scientist explain the subtle connections between the various biological units of a human body and their functions, one cannot but be moved to the point of feeling tender towards this wonderful mechanism. Our bodies do put up with all kinds of abuse, physical and mental, for 60, 70 or 80 years, and complain only when the misuse has gone too far. The somewhat sensitive people, who stop abusing the body before the no-return point is reached, are rewarded with rejuvenation by the hidden intelligence and the constructive forces of the biological system. It may be said that, in most people, the body is doing a thankless job. Over and above this is the deplorable issue of committing suicide, punishing the body to have the satisfaction of taking revenge on somebody or to end one's own overwhelming self-pity. People who go through a near death experience after an attempted suicide return to tell us that this anticipated satisfaction is one of gross illusion and that the intended target is never reached by that senseless approach. When this truth reaches the gut feeling of human beings, there will be significant reduction in suicides.

In the Bhagavad Gita, Krishna says that the human body is like a boat primarily meant to carry us across the ocean of life and death to the shores of immortality. We certainly don't want to travel by a leaky boat! The simile of the boat applies to both 'Stula Sareera,' the physical body, and 'Sookshma Sareera,' the subtle body. During the discarnate period, we are carried on by the subtle body. In this chapter, we focus on the physical body.

In the Esoteric Field, the human mind, freed from its conditioning to some extent at least, feels tender towards everything; even towards the so-called inanimate things. That being so, it is needless to say that under those circumstances the human body receives the care and attention that it deserves. Regarding this heightened sensitivity towards everything in the world, there is a nice passage in *Siddhartha* by Hermann Hesse (Hesse, 1993). The story has it that enlightenment takes place in Siddhartha, the hero of the story, after he goes through many experiences, some of them deeply saddening. In the evening of his life, when he functions as an old ferryman across a river, he meets his young days' friend Govinda who happens to be on his way across that river. The two spend some time together in the wooded ambience reminiscing about their young days. Asked to explain his inner discoveries, Siddhartha gives a moving description of the state of mind in which pervasive consciousness unites one with everything in the universe. During that description, Siddhartha picks up a stone and says that he respects it not so much because it will evolve and become a human being and eventually a Buddha but because it contains all of it in its essence even now and, for the time being, it appears to be a stone. This kind of respect for everything *per se* begins to impact the mind in the Esoteric Field, as outlined in chapter 5.

The Practical Side

There are six main avenues along which attention to health can be directed. People are familiar with these avenues but, quite often, do not apply themselves seriously to them; life is too busy professionally, socially and otherwise. Once they understand the intrinsic value of robust health, they somehow find time for attention to the six avenues and they move on to a stable track. Those avenues are:

1. Diet and Dietary Supplements
2. Sleep (Duration and Quality)
3. Yoga and Exercise
4. Games and Sports
5. Hobbies
6. Leisure

There are many good books on the market that tell us how we can gainfully apply ourselves to those items. So, in this book, we will not dwell on the conventional aspects but touch upon a few items that don't usually find a place in literature. Thus, only some issues in the above list will find a place here. The apparently contradictory mixture of seriousness and lighthearted attitudes helps us sail smoothly towards good health. Some involvement of the spirit of adventure is involved; those interested will discover this through their own reflections.

Dietary Supplements: Apart from a wholesome diet, a few supplements can help us maintain good health. These include items like the various vitamins, calcium, honey, dry fruits such as dates and raisins, peanuts, almonds and so on. There are also some herbal preparations tested over long periods of time. It is part of the adventure to look around for these supplements. Needless to say, that any such acrobatics with the supplements should be tried only under the guidance of a family physician. It is wise to have a second opinion too. Make sure, in the first place, that the one you are consulting is taking those supplements! Further, whatever we consume that way should be given a 'drug holiday,' as the medical field calls it. This means that we don't take them too regularly for too long a time but give them an appropriate break frequently. This moratorium on the intake ensures that the body gets a chance to flush out the unwanted accumulations, so they don't end up as silent poisons.

Overenthusiasm about good health can land us in trouble. Some years ago, Robert Benchley wrote a humorous article in *Reader's Digest* on phobias. His imaginativeness in defining strange fears and giving them funny titles of phobias make the article hilarious. Robert says that there is a phobia whereby the affected person is afraid of falling in front of the chair because he is sitting too much in front. So, the person keeps kicking himself backwards until he tips over and falls on the rear side! This is an apt metaphor for those who become overenthusiastic about good health. We may keep dumping vitamins into our body until hypervitaminosis throws us down backwards! Obviously, we must know when to stop. But how does one know how much is too much? Understandably, we have to be inquisitive and trust our 'grey cells.' In the book *The Treasured Writings of Kahlil Gibran* (Gibran, 1998), Kahlil says, "After 30, the best doctor for you is yourself."

By the way, in the above spoof on phobias, Robert discusses many fears, half of them configured by his fertile imagination. It is so well written that you keep laughing through it to the point your real phobias don't seem to matter! Towards the end of his essay, he tickles us by saying, "If you tell us what your phobia is, we will tell you what you are afraid of"! Isn't that cute? Surely, such humor keeps us in good health!

Sleep: Sleep! Yes, we all love it. However, not many of us give it an affectionate hug. Rather, it is gone through as a matter of course. We have more important things to do: E-mails to reply, bills to be paid, papers to file, deadlines to be met, the dog to be taken to the vet and so on. Added to it, maybe there is a list of engagements from the spouse! In addition, you are perhaps busy writing a book on how to find leisure. The result: Sleep becomes the first casualty. So long as sleep is treated as a secondary thing, it is unlikely that one becomes interested in the esoteric matters. Once a person is drawn to the region outside the common rut, there is a natural pull towards respecting sleep as an honored facet of life. This does not mean wallowing in laziness by extending the hours of sleep. It means one understands the content of sleep as a life-preserver and respects its nuances in terms of quantity and quality. It leads one to appreciate the sublime role that sleep plays in our biorhythm.

How much attention do we pay to making the bed? Does the linen in contact with the body get washed frequently? With what care do we prepare the elements? Are the bed, the pillows and sheets homologous with the natural profile of the body while asleep? Is the bedroom well ventilated? Is it dark enough and noise free? After having food, does enough time elapse before going to sleep? Do we unburden all our mental loads before falling asleep? Is one calm enough to watch sleep entering the body?

Three types of consciousness are recognized in human beings: In Sanskrit, they are termed as:

1. Susupthi, the deep dreamless sleep
2. Swapna, the dreaming state, known commonly as the rapid eye movement (REM) period
3. Jaagrat, the wakeful state

It is during Susupthi that the body gets its full rejuvenating time. The longer this period, the better. One can explore ways of extending the Susupthi hours. Rejuvenation proceeds probably even during the Swapna period but perhaps with less efficacy. However, it has been found that Swapna helps the brain to shed some of its stress. During Jaagrat both the body and mind are active and so they do not get enough rest. The tendency is more towards being stressed. Instead of being de-stressed, they become distressed!

According to some studies, it is known that the body sleeps soundly for the first three hours followed by two hours of light sleep and then again by three hours of deep sleep. It is good to adjust our hours such that we wake up during the light-sleep periods. Usually, the human body needs eight hours of sleep every day. Contingencies in modern living may not always permit these to be carried out satisfactorily. All one can do is to avoid the avoidable. Whenever one is unable to fulfill those expectations, it is good to make amends for the lapse at the earliest opportunity.

If some persistent extraneous noise disturbs the sleep, one may try the approach of creating 'white noise' in the bedroom. White noise is of a steady tone at some acceptable decibel level that smudges the disturbing noise; that is, drowns the intruder! This is based on the fact that the brain does not get disturbed by steady noise even if it is louder than the intruder because the intruder has sharp peaks. White noise can be created by attaching a piece of paper to the back of a table-fan and letting it flutter. Fine tuning the paper-flutter to produce the required level of white noise is a matter of fun. Such a suggestion may appear a little crazy but it has worked admirably for some people. The writer has been significantly benefited by it on several occasions when the extraneous noise drove him up the wall. Helped by the white noise, he came down and slept well. He was pleasantly surprised to find the same suggestion being given by the author of an article in *Reader's Digest*. That author recommends, as a second alternative, switching on a radio and tuning it to a non-station frequency. Here, of course, we have better control over adjusting the white noise level.

The idea of making additional noise in the room may not appeal to some. Jerome K. Jerome wrote, in his humorous book *Three Men in a Boat* (Jerome, 1900), that one of his friends complained of headache. Another friend offered to play the banjo to soothe his nerves. But the first friend said, "No, I prefer the headache"! In that manner, people may prefer to leave the disturbing noise as it is and not have something rattling about in the bedroom to smother the intruder. It depends on the individual. All we can say is: Give this matter of white noise a sincere try and see if you prefer the headache or the banjo.

In any case, once you apply yourself to the matter of sleep as a venerable issue, you begin to discover things on your own. It is part of self-discovery resulting from expanding awareness. The problem of insomnia has to be approached from the medical point of view as well as from the issue of the noisy mind. In this connection, you may recall the value of Bardo mentioned in chapter 8. During the Bardo period, if one is quietly self-aware, one can sense consciousness converging toward the Heart Center, one of the seven Chakras. It is a good feeling. The deeper you move into the Esoteric Field, the lesser is the problem of insomnia.

Yoga and Exercise: A great deal of information is available from literature on these loveable items. Here we look into some unconventional aspects only. It is good to know that, in the region of yoga and exercise, there is a possibility of overindulgence and, consequently, hurting oneself. Moderation is the watchword. For example, excessive jogging or tennis may wear out the knees well before old age. So, we notice that there is such a thing as keeping the body well preserved. A harmonious balance between exercising and preserving deserves attention. Not much is written about the second aspect. This is where special care is needed and one can be creative.

In 1976, Therese Bertherat and Carol Bernstein published a book in French which was later translated into English with the title *The Body Has Its Reasons* (Bertherat and Bernstein, 1976). Its subtitle is: Anti-Exercises and Self-Awareness. A comment on the back cover says: "A remarkable book; the marvelous new route to Total Body Awareness." That book is full of unconventional ways of treating the body. It can help us discover a new approach to body care. In it, the 'well preserved' aspect is given attention.

Of late, more people are taking to walking as a wholesome exercise. It wears out the body less compared to some vigorous exercises and, hence, the preservation aspect is fulfilled. Quite a few of us would have seen the one-page bunch of advice under the caption *Desiderata*, either in a shop or in a friend's house. We feel good in going through that presentation. An important line there is: Beyond a wholesome discipline, be gentle with yourself.

Yoga should not be treated merely as a matter of twisted bodily positions. The state of mind during the asana (the posture) is important. Our minds usually go 'wool-gathering' while the body remains still in its final position of an asana. Attempting to control the mind cannot help. That can only lead to conflict and a tense situation. What is meaningful is to be quietly self-aware of the noisy mind and its proclivity to wander off during that time. Not to fight with the mind is to be a friend of it and, in that friendly atmosphere, something can take place. This passive attention to the mind during the yoga is not usually emphasized and given the importance that it deserves.

Another healthy aspect of yoga is that one should not be too rigid about the instructions received. Here too it is good to explore one's own natural inclinations and allow for flexibility. This is where one can learn what it means to listen to the body and follow its instructions. That way we pay attention to the inner Guru who is superior to the outer Gurus. This statement may sound blasphemous to some people but then no insult is meant to the human Gurus. They do help us a great deal in learning yoga and other spiritual things, and so they deserve due respect. While being grateful to them, we notice that a mere conformist attitude cannot take us deep into the realm of yoga. After they give us the initial push, we must be free to take the journey by ourselves towards the inner Guru. Moving towards the inner Guru is the ultimate objective of yoga. Thus, while following the overall instructions on doing yogasanas, it is good to know how to listen to the body and introduce one's own variations in the postures. These variations may suggest themselves only once in a while but we must remain open to them. This creative approach helps us understand the value of spontaneity in yogic awareness which serves as an aid to the Radial Dive. It can make yoga sessions very refreshing apart from helping us receive the usual dividends in the realm of physical health. The sessions must be enjoyable and not be a period of struggle.

There are two items that may be termed 'anti-yoga.' They are: Standing or talking for long periods at a stretch. Avoiding these 'anti-yoga' items is as important, if not more important, than doing yoga! Self-awareness helps us discover other anti-yoga items in daily life and so, in that very process, free ourselves from them.

The Second Line

Now we come to an important concept of health in the name of 'the Second Line.' It can help us understand the state of our body in terms of its heightened or lessened well-being. Once we become familiar with this concept, it functions like a gauge in assessing the body's state of health. Now, we study the graph below.

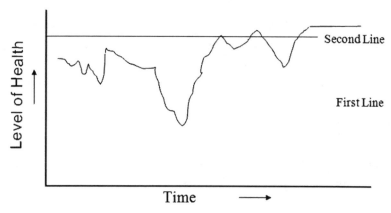

Fig. 10 Fluctuation in Health with Time

In Fig. 10, the changing level of health is plotted against time. The First Line indicates a level below which the body falls sick. The farther we are below that line, the more the body is unwell. (If we fall all the way down to the bottom line, we are dead.

God forbid!) Once we are cured of the illness, we rise above the First Line. The higher we are above that line, the healthier we feel. At the level of the Second Line, there is a distinct feeling of heightened physical well-being. Above this, the euphoria progressively increases.

Normally, we are satisfied to be above the First Line. 'So long as I am not sick, it is okay.' With some additional care, we rise in the level of health and come closer to the Second Line. On falling sick, we become conscious of our body. Generally, when our health is in the region between the First and Second Lines, we are not aware of the body. On rising to the Second Line and above, we again become conscious of the body, but now with the feeling of wellness. In fact, it is this euphoric feeling in sensing the wellness that functions as the signal telling us that we are at the second level. This holistic bodily awareness is characteristic of the health levels on and above the Second Line. We notice that if we keep ourselves at that level, the probability of falling sick becomes low, because it is quite a distance to go down. In other words, our resistance to sickness increases. Viruses may be going round, bacteria may be dancing around, but they don't capture us. Even simple illnesses like the common cold, headache and fever do not bother a person in the region above the Second Line; that is the nature of the metabolic robustness prevailing in that region. Apart from not easily falling sick, we enjoy just being alive if we are at the higher health levels. You may call the level of the Second Line the Feather Health Level, because there we feel so light. Being of such high quality, it can only be reached with some dedication. One of the obstacles to it is the tendency to feel satisfied in just not being sick.

Those interested in rising to the Second Line begin to understand the major and minor abuses to which we usually subject the body. That is the first step. Then we take note of those items that significantly contribute to good health. With that kind of interest, sooner or later we climb to the second level, sense its beauty and stay there.

In the early stages of reaching the second level we may frequently fall below it but, with sustained interest and application, it becomes easy to remain constantly above the Second Line. One gets the feeling that the 'Susupthi' period is extended. Dreams begin to toe the frivolous line and become less and less disturbing. The body's intelligence is happy to function at its best. The aging process slows down.

The Third Line

Perhaps there are some more lines above the Second Line which can be lived with intensity. However, we have to go up gradually feeling our way through each line. To many people, even the idea of the Second Line will appear phony, merely a theoretical idea. You probably hear someone say, "The writer's imagination has gone berserk!" If, however, you feel that this matter of the Second Line touches a deep chord in you, then you can explore that and the lines above it.

The Second Line is characterized by harmony of the physical system. With deeper attention to living as a whole, the vista expands. One begins to sense the close link between the body and the mind and hence becomes interested in their interactive harmony. Attention focuses on the psycho-physical system as a single unit. This frees the mind from being embroiled in its own self-centered activities. Silence descends on the system. Love, the expression of the soul, begins to flow towards everyone and everything. The exalted Third Line is endowed with that kind of wholesomeness.

Without a stable residence above the Second Line, it is unlikely that the significance of the Third Line is felt. However, feeling drawn towards the Third Line at any stage has a meaningful value. That line signifies a synergistic confluence of a calm mind and a healthy body. Orderliness in daily life becomes a natural consequence. There will be no need to fight habits or addictions. Loneliness, boredom, persecution complex and the like quit forever. Empathy rules, not emotion. People who have a near death experience report a quality of peacefulness and abundant feeling for all aspects of life. Near the Third Line, those qualities begin to dawn in one's life even without a paranormal experience. The cosmological significance of our existence and proximity to Divinity are felt beyond all ego-satisfying religious and philosophical concepts. Self-centered activities related to personal salvation drop off.

The Third Line is associated with a merger of physical and psychological energies that moves us towards the cosmic oneness of all things. One gets a feeling of the stillness in which the primal energy and intelligence take repose. The associated witness consciousness is the one that releases us from both the body and the mind. There is a feeling of the affectionate bystander attitude and a touch of the ancient; that awareness takes us towards the Primal Self.

The Fourth Line

Thank God, there is no Fourth Line! If you discover one, let us, your fellow passengers on life's journey, know about it before you are attracted to the Fifth Line.

In any case, we do notice that starting from simple attention to good health, there are many heights to be scaled. In this respect, life throws its gauntlet at us affectionately. Let us pick it up with confidence and win too!

Chapter 11

Childlikeness

Whenever somebody uses the word childlike, it is always greeted by all with a smile that is childlike! Imbued with curiosity and innocence, childlikeness has a heart-warming quality. Once the mind becomes interested in self-awareness and is attracted to the esoteric aspects of life's journey, childlikeness begins to express itself in its own way. This is particularly noticed in the salient features of child psychology: wonderment, inquisitive attitudes and a spirit of adventure. Not building up rancor or vengeful attitudes is certainly a part of it. Cheerfulness too is endemic to that psychology. Wouldn't it be wonderful to let those qualities keep us company even as we grow up and get caught in the humdrum of life? It is easier said than done because, on this planet, the onslaught of life that we go through can indeed be oppressive and may dash out the child in us. What is it that can let the child sustain itself in our psychology? When we grown-ups find the answer to this question, we can let the young ones imbibe that quality early in their lives. Indeed, it is contagious. Childlikeness is a good pointer towards a vibrant life. Jesus is reported to have said, "Until ye become like children, ye cannot enter heaven."

We have to remind ourselves now and then that an important objective of this book is to understand the value of some hidden items and let it transpire in us in its own way. Exerting effort or struggling to bring it about cannot help. It is an elusive art and our application in that direction makes us grow in confidence and be at ease with ourselves.

Taking It Easy

A dictionary (Thorndike and Barnhart, 1983) defines the word childlike as *innocent, frank, simple* and then gives an example: *He has a childlike love of the circus.* If an adult goes to attend a circus all by oneself, that person is likely to be ridiculed. But as the dictionary points out, that is an example of childlikeness in a person. This does not mean that we should be attending every circus in the town year-round in order to prove to ourselves that we are childlike! Suffice it to give the natural inclination in us a free rope towards fascinating things. Incidentally, an act in the circus may kindle our interest to try it out, and we would soon be amusing ourselves in becoming a triumphant amateur of that act; may even grow to be an adept at it. Such indulgences can help us foster the child in us amidst our workaday involvements.

As we all know, juggling is one thing that is fascinating to watch. The imaginativeness in formulating the nuances of the act, apart from the act itself, adds to the fascination. Then there is this item of walking on tall stilts. The person is kept from falling down by the long swing of the stilts that generates the required gyroscopic momentum. Apparently, the artist's feet are secured firmly to the stilts. (Otherwise, the stilts may come off at the most inopportune moment and cause an embarrassing collapse.) With that kind of immobility between his feet and the stilts, one wonders how this person gets off at the end of the act. Usually, he disappears into the greenroom towards the end. Does he hold on to something, abandoning the stilts, before getting down? In that case, the stilts may go awry and taunt him! Do some volunteers rush to release him from those blessed stilts? There seems to be some mystery surrounding the end of the act. It would also be interesting to see how he got on to them in the first place!

Lighthearted attitudes always help us keep our balance. An automobile mechanic was once asked how to handle unexpected problems that stall the car on a highway. He laughed and said,

"All you need is a sense of humor. Things will work out your way!" (This should, no doubt, be combined with practical wisdom that would obviate the occurrence of automobile problems on the way.) Much of what transpires outside is related to what transpires inside us. Humorists and comedians keep reminding us about the light side of life. Joviality, mirthfulness and nonchalance seem to play a role in childlikeness.

We meet a few people among our relatives and friends who seem to sustain cheerfulness and lighthearted attitudes, notwithstanding gnawing problems in their lives. They make us feel good when they are around. Obviously, the child in them is alive. When we encourage young students in their inquisitiveness, in their spirit of adventure, we are likely to help them grow into cheerful beings. For that to happen, those inclinations must be a part of our own psychology and express themselves in our own interactions.

Wonderment

For those interested in the esoteric aspects of life, wonderment often plays a role in their observation on life, body and mind. The inner dive sustains that feeling, and childlikeness has something to do with it. Strangely, this is also the driving force behind scientific discoveries. During near death experiences (NDEs), wonderment seems to reach high levels. In the Esoteric Field, the feeling of wonderment is the one that keeps the explorer's inquisitive attitudes alive and prevents one from clinging to beliefs or disbelief. This open-mindedness is necessary for inward, non-verbal discoveries. It is good to understand the value of and the content of wonderment.

Jean Ritchie has a chapter with the heading "Light Shines for Children" in her book *Death's Door* (Ritchie, 1996). She says that children are the best witnesses for the phenomenon of near death experience, because their minds are uncluttered, unprejudiced and uninfluenced by culture. She mentions that

Dr. Melvin Morse, an American pediatrician, studied such experiences in children (Morse, 1992). Dr. Morse points out that children are filled with wonder without a lot of interpretation. The abominable tendency of the merely rational mind to explain away things does not operate in them and the experience remains deeply etched in their memory for the rest of their lives.

The Universe is full of mysteries and, like a kind mother, it waits patiently for us to grow in our awareness to be able to perceive and appreciate those things. Albert Einstein is reported to have said, "Wonderment is the source of all true art and all science. He to whom this emotion is a stranger, who can no longer pause to wonder and stand rapt in awe, is as good as dead; his eyes are closed." It is likely that those who are drawn to wondering will see or sense things that others remain unaware of. They learn that when they give free rein to the movement of wonder in them, there is a possibility that they uncover life's deeper mysteries. That in itself is a matter of expanding awareness. It has something to do with childlikeness.

Looking at things that have happened in the past centuries, we wonder at the way man has risen in his knowledge of the Earth and the Universe. We feel superior to our ancestors in our advancement but it also means that our descendants will know more than us. Where is the end? It is shrouded in mystery. Regarding the past, Heinz Haber gives some interesting anecdotes in his book *Stars, Men and Atoms* (Haber, 1963). He says that even in the days of Columbus many intelligent people could not conceive of the spherical shape of the Earth. While expecting approval for his plan from the court of Spain for trying a new route to India sailing westward, he had to face an argument: *"What will happen to you when you reach the end of the world? Will not your ships go over the rim and plunge into the dark abyss?"* We smile at this vacuum in their knowledge but, some centuries ahead of us now, we may face the same fate with regard to the ideas that we hold at present. There is a feeling of wonderment on how long this can go on. It releases us from the superciliousness that human beings tend to ride on because of the rise in knowledge. The ensuing detachment is helpful in moving one inward, a journey towards intrinsic awareness that is untouched by the outer processes. Perhaps, that awareness contains the answers to all questions.

Hubert Reeves, author of *Atoms of Silence* (Reeves, 1984), says in that book on astronomy that he dedicates his book to all those who marvel at the Universe. It is a matter of unending expansion of our consciousness. Those are the times when we step out of the psychological cage that we build around ourselves. There are some TV shows, such as those of the Discovery Channel, which take us to the wilderness in different parts of the world. If we can listen to them with some intimate feelings, we go outside the cage and sense the mysterious nature of Nature! Again, proximity to Divinity is felt through Direct Awareness, unsullied by religious beliefs. Love, the language of the soul, begins to express itself. The fellow passengers of our journey of life get some attention from us.

People who are interested in leading a vibrant life are always attracted to the item of solving puzzles. A mind concentrating on unraveling a puzzle is temporarily freed from the ego. For that time being it is functioning from outside the knots mentioned in chapter 4. There is also the fact that Athma Vichara (the Soul Search) treads on similar grounds in the sense of being inquisitive and ready to face a challenge. As mentioned before, the field of science proceeds the same way. No doubt, Athma Vichara goes beyond the merely logical approach and relies, in addition, on Direct Awareness. It is good to observe the state of mind when it is solving a puzzle. That awareness can be quite interesting.

The book *Figures for Fun* by Yakov Perelman is one of many books that come up with interesting puzzles (Perelman, 1979). There is a mind-boggling item in that book regarding the amount of wheat grains requested by a wise man whom the king wanted to reward for his invention of the game of chess. The inventor said he would like to have an amount of wheat that would fill the chess board in the manner of one grain in the first square, two in the second, four in the third, eight in the fourth and so on up to the 64 squares. The king thought it was a pittance and so he promised to deliver the grains in the evening. By that time the king's associates found that the total amount of grains satisfying the requested pile was not available in the whole of their kingdom, not even in the whole world! Perelman makes an interesting calculation. He asks: "If we have a box with a cross section of 4 meters by 10 meters cross section, what length of the box would be required to contain all those grains?" It turns out that the length required is the distance to the Sun from the Earth and back! This is about three hundred million kilometers. When we hear it for the first time, we miss a heartbeat. Could any of us have imagined that? It shows that the mind can be tripped by its own limitations in judging. If that is the case with an objective issue of volume calculation, what to speak of the subjective matters!

The Pointers from Stories

Quite a few stories and movies have an esoteric import. They move us into pensive moods and make us look at things that we would have otherwise missed. Reflection on those items can reveal some hidden aspects that can help deepen our self-awareness.

As children, we have all enjoyed the comics: Stories through pictures. Some of the earliest ones in this regard appeared in the twentieth century; for example, the stories of Tarzan and the Phantom. One reason why they were so interesting is that they were set in a jungle ambience, with a strange atmosphere of the unknown. That took us closer to Nature. Further, they had a touch of the mysterious and of the eerie. The inner dive always makes us love nature and be interested in what lies beyond the apparent. So, the above stories have a subconscious appeal. Tarzan and the Phantom are animal lovers. That also adds to the appeal. When we hear that Tarzan could talk to the elephant, the ape and other animals, it stirs something deep in us. Silence of the forest has a penetrative quality and the silence of our hearts resonates with the silence of the forest. Modern life alienates us from those intimate feelings, though some aspects of that life are exceptions. As children we enjoyed the stories in one way, but as grown-ups the impact on us is different. Now they can have a philosophic import. Some jungle pictures in the comics can open a path into our inner realms if we accept their invitations.

In one of the stories, Tarzan faces perilous hostility from jungle tribes in his attempt to rescue a small group of Europeans from them. By his clever and courageous ways, he succeeds and brings the Europeans on an elephant to the edge of the forest from where they could safely return home. As Tarzan was about to depart to his jungle quarters on the elephant back, one in the group gratefully remarks, "Tarzan, we don't find enough words to thank you." And Tarzan says, "There is no need. The eyes meet and the hearts understand. That is enough." It is clear that, when the heart functions, insistence on outward norms and expressions are unnecessary. There are many aspects of the Tarzan stories that tend to remain with us forever. They function as mild pointers towards childlike appreciation of the journey of life.

What would it be like to stay in Tarzan's treehouse atop the foliage? To lie there in the night and listen to the deep-throated calls of animals and other creatures can be quite an experience. But we won't like the idea because it is difficult to get an Internet connection in that God-forsaken place! The funny part is that, if ever God forsakes a place, it will be our cities and not the jungles. There are places in the world, such as the Serengeti

Plains in Africa, where lodges are set amidst the vast areas of animal roaming grounds. When we stay there and listen to the groans of the wildlife in the night, it stirs something deep in our consciousness. Perhaps they take us back to the ancient days of man when he lived in intimate contact with nature and animals.

As expounded in the heritage of India, the three significant Gunas (characteristics or mental streams) of human beings fall along the following three categories:

1. Saatvic – virtuous and gentle
2. Rajasic – energetic and active
3. Tamasic – idle and inertial

Krishna says in the Bhagavad Gita that the forest is the Saatvica dwelling, the town is the Rajasica dwelling, and the gambling den that of the Tamasica. Thus, the forest seems to get a nod from Krishna as an exalted place.

One would like to wear a protective outfit and have a playful combat with a cheetah. It would require a mind that is totally free of fear. Otherwise, the fear in our minds will trigger the fear in the animal and the related aggression. An incident which took place in Ramanasramam (the hermitage in Tiruvannamalai, Tamil Nadu, India), where Ramana Maharishi lived, is relevant here. (Maharishi in Sanskrit means an exalted sage.) People from the West visited Ramana Maharishi during the early part of the twentieth century. The ashram used to be the meeting place of the aspirants for Truth. Paul Brunton, a British journalist, spent some time at the ashram. Desiring to have tea one afternoon, he returned to his hut set amidst wooded surroundings. When he opened the door, he was taken aback by a slithering movement close to his feet. It was a cobra! He drew back with a rush and shouted. Soon a sage-like person appeared behind him, went ahead of him and approached the snake, holding out his hands towards it. Wonderstruck, the Westerner watched the snake bend its head before the newcomer who then gently stroked the cobra's tail. The snake remained calm until it saw others coming. Then, with a quick slithering movement, it left the hut and disappeared into the jungle bush. Paul Brunton was told that the person who stroked the cobra was Yogi Ramiah, a long-term associate of Ramana Maharishi. When Brunton had a later occasion to ask the yogi about the cobra incident, the yogi said that he had no fear in his mind and that he approached it without hatred and with love in his heart for all beings. Brunton explains all this in graphic detail in his book *A Search In Secret India* (Brunton, 1970). That book was originally published in 1934 in England and later in America.

We now again return to the jungle heroes. In a story of the Phantom by Lee Falk, the hero was to round up a bunch of pirates who had just recently indulged in an abominable looting of a ship and its passengers. Subsequently, those pirates spilled over and got lost in the crowds of the coastal town where the ship halted. Phantom's efforts to locate them did not succeed. So, he told himself, "If you cannot find them, let them find you." Then he did some clever things. The pirates found their way to him and got caught. The point here is that, strangely, Athma Vichara strikes a parallel; we cannot chase and find the ultimate Truth. All one can do is to remove the obstacles and lie fallow. The Truth will flood in at its own time, in its own way. A statement of Jesus is pertinent here: The Kingdom of God will not happen if you are looking for it. You read this in the book *The Gospel According to Jesus* (Mitchell, 1943).

Sir Arthur Conan Doyle's stories of Sherlock Holmes are well known for the skills in detection as well as for some thrilling scenarios. His characterization of Holmes has several fine points to it. The detective's confidence, dedication and spirited application are some of those. Compassion too expresses itself through the windows that open amidst his smartness. That is what distinguishes him from merely being an efficient robot. We cannot imitate him or try to emulate his qualities. That will only lead to yet another self-centered activity. When we understand their content and see the beauty in them, they may manifest in us in their own way.

Thrilling moments reach a crescendo in quite a few of Holmes' adventures. If we dwell on the eerie feelings of those occasions, they can open a door into our inner realms. Take for example the story with the title *Adventure of the Speckled Band*. It is that part of the story where Holmes is about to zero in on the culprit and beard the lion in its den. Holmes and his friend Watson have to take a train to reach the railway station near the culprit's place. They travel with a heavy heart because their client, a lady, was in imminent danger of being murdered by the culprit, her stepfather. The scene for it was being set in an atmosphere of mystery and awe. At that point, the following lines appear in the story as narrated by Dr. Watson, Holmes' associate. The eerie trend in the story gradually gathers momentum.

At Waterloo we were fortunate in catching a train to Leatherhead, where we hired a trap at the station inn and drove for four or five miles through the lovely Surrey lanes. It was a perfect day, with a bright sun and a few fleecy clouds in the heavens. The trees and the wayside hedges were just throwing out their first green shoots, and the air was full of the pleasant smell of moist earth. To me at least there was a strange contrast between the sweet promise of the spring and this sinister quest upon which we were engaged.

The two friends then stay at an inn, not too far from the culprit's house. They are supposed to get a signal (by a light being placed in the window) from the client towards midnight when all falls quiet in the house. Then they will move to the house and keep a nocturnal vigil to lay open the culprit's evil designs. At this point, suspense rides high through the following lines.

> About nine o'clock, the light among the trees was extinguished and all was dark in the direction of the Manor House. Two hours passed by slowly, and then, suddenly at the stroke of eleven, a single bright light shone out right in front of us.
>
> "That is our signal," said Holmes springing to his feet. "It comes from the middle window."
>
> As we passed out, he exchanged a few words with the landlord, explaining that we were going on a late-night visit to an acquaintance, and that it was possible that we might spend the night there. A moment later we were out on the dark road, a chill wind blowing in our faces, and one yellow light twinkling in front of us through the gloom to guide us on our somber errand.

And so goes the story with the suspense growing in intensity line by line after the above scenario. The pointer here lies in our state of mind as it goes through such eerie moments. Attraction to the esoteric side of life can be a characteristic of that state if we pay passionate attention to those moments. There seems to be some secret shrouded in it that can lead us to a door in the wall we build around us.

The Pointers from Essays

Some authors touch us deeply with their essays; deeply in the sense of making us dwell on the hidden sentiments of life. They help us jump out of the rut that we unknowingly keep deepening with our habitual thought. In that sense, those essays help us move into the Esoteric Field in some way.

Here we look at an example. Jerome K. Jerome, the English author, is known for his humorous writings. The philosophic content that runs parallel to his humor is what makes his presentation penetrative. This is particularly evident in his book *Idle Thoughts of an Idle Fellow* (Jerome, 1903). The absence of that book may create a lacuna in the shelf of every spirited person. In one of the essays in that book, with the caption "On Babies," he mentions jocularly all the pranks and mischief that children indulge in, and then the following poignant lines come in tandem.

But there, there, there! I shall get myself the character of a baby-hater if I talk any more in that strain. And Heaven knows I am not one. Who could be, to look into the innocent faces clustered in timid helplessness round those great gates that open down into the world?

The world, the small round world! What a vast mysterious place it must seem to baby eyes! What a trackless continent the back garden appears! What marvelous explorations they make in the cellar under the stairs! With what awe they gaze down the long street, wondering, like us bigger babies when we gaze up at the stars, where it all ends!

And down the longest street of all, that long, dim street of life that stretches out before them, what grave old-fashioned looks they seem to cast! What pitiful, frightened looks sometimes! I saw a little mite sitting on a doorstep in a Soho slum one night, and I shall never forget the look that the gas lamp showed me on its wizen face, a look of dull despair, as if from the squalid court the vista of its own squalid life had risen, ghost-like, and struck its heart dead with horror.

Poor little feet, just commencing the stony journey! We old travelers, far down the road, can only pass to wave a hand to you. You come out of the dark mist, and we, looking back, so tiny in the distance, standing on the brow of the hill, your arms stretched out toward us. God speed you! We would like to stay a while longer and take your little hands in ours, but the murmur of the great sea is in our ears and we may not linger. We must hasten down, for the shadowy ships are waiting to spread their sable sails.

There is a similar passage that touches our hearts in the essay with the title "On Cats and Dogs." Again, after a humorous and poignant presentation on the association of human beings with these pets, Jerome writes some moving lines worth reflecting on. They follow after his musings on rats. He says that the poor rats seem only to exist so that cats and dogs may gain credit for killing them and chemists make a fortune by inventing specialties in poison for their destruction. He feels there is something fascinating about the rats along lines of being weird and uncanny. After giving examples for these, he goes on to the melancholic story of the Pied Piper of Hamelin. Using the stream of the story as a base, Jerome paints a moving scenario of human life on this planet, as revealed by the following lines:

Then there is the story of the Pied Piper of Hamelin; how he first piped the rats away, and afterwards, when the mayor broke faith with him, drew all the children along with him and went into the mountain. What a curious old legend that is! I wonder what it means, or has it any meaning at all. There seems to be something deep, lying hidden beneath the rippling rhyme. It haunts me, that picture of the quaint, mysterious old piper piping through Hamelin's narrow streets, and the children following with dancing feet and thoughtful, eager faces. The old folks try to stay them, but the children pay no heed. They hear the weird, witched music and must follow. The games are left unfinished and the playthings drop from their careless hands. They know not whither they are hastening. The mystic music calls to them, and they follow, heedless and unasking where. It stirs and vibrates in their hearts and other sounds grow faint. So, they wander through Pied Piper Street away from Hamelin town (to be lost forever).

I get to think sometimes if the Pied Piper is really dead, or if he may not still be roaming up and down our streets and lanes, but playing now so softly that only the children can hear him. Why do the little faces look so grave and solemn when they pass awhile from romping, and stand, deep wrapped, with straining eyes? They only shake their curly heads and dart back laughing to their playmates when we question them. But I fancy myself they have been listening to the magic music of the old Pied Piper, and perhaps with those bright eyes of theirs have even seen his odd, fantastic figure gliding unnoticed through the whirl and throng.

Even we grown-up children hear his piping now and then. But the yearning notes are far away, and the noisy, blustering world is always bellowing so loud it drowns the dream-like melody. One day the sweet, sad strains will sound out full and clear, and then we too shall, like the little children, throw our playthings all aside and follow. The loving hands will be stretched out to stay us, and the voices we have learnt to listen to will cry to us to stop. But we shall push the fond arms gently back and pass out through the sorrowing house and through the open door. For the wild, strange music will be ringing in our hearts, and we shall know the meaning of it by then.

Every time one reads it, one's eyes well up in tears. Like Jerome, there are other authors who invite us to visit those hidden corners of our hearts. We do not normally dwell on such deeply touching presentations long enough, and often enough, for them to make inroads into us and bring about a lasting change in our psychology. They have the power to widen our perspective and to make us move towards the Inner Being.

Chapter 12

This Matter of Dos & Don'ts

When people become somewhat serious and want to get a grip on their lives, they look around for being guided by Dos and Don'ts. Almost all the books on the market that deal with the human mind and life focus on giving the reader instructions on what to do and not to do. This seems so natural that the authors and the readers form a cogent pair in this matter. Religious preachers also toe that line. Perhaps, the reader is tempted to ask, "What is wrong with that?" The following paragraphs say something about it.

If you listen to an Enlightened Master speak, you notice that the talk rarely rides on Dos and Don'ts. Such talks are not addressed to the outer self but to the Deeper being so that the growing awareness in the listener gets charged, and there is nothing for the ego to hold on to. If you take notes during the talk, the Master usually discourages such a thing because the one that wants to gain something in the future is the outer self, the ego. The Master's talks are in the form of an exposition that lights the way even as one listens, a matter of transformation in the very act of listening. They do not say anything about what one should or should not do. They describe the actuality and, sensing that during the listening, inner transformation takes place of its own accord. Some listeners, however, tend to cull out Dos and Don'ts even from such presentations and try to practice them. Sooner or later, they would see the absurdity of that approach. People in whom awareness has advanced to some extent listen quietly to the Master and, riding on his words, enter the void within. The literal content of the Master's words does not block them. Even while listening, they sense the intrinsic beauty of the inner silence. As we go along that way, we realize the absurdity of asking, "How am I to continue in that silence?", as that is the very proclivity of the ego. A good listener knows that the Master's talk takes one unobtrusively along the Radial Dive. Deep inner peace reigns during the talk. However, one is likely to be thrown athwart as soon as the usual humdrum of daily life takes over. For example, the next day after listening to the talk, one may have a raucous quarrel with the boss in the office! What went wrong? Yesterday's peace seems to have gone to pieces! One wonders, and this curiosity is part of the growing awareness. There is no guilty feeling and the whole thing is looked upon as a matter of ridiculous fun. The inner voice says, "Take it easy." With such lightheartedness, one finds oneself cracking jokes with the boss the next day, over a cup of coffee at the office cafeteria! It is this nonchalance and childlikeness that is the key to Radical Transformation. In contrast, one who values a moralizing speech is likely to feel very guilty if he does a Don't and doesn't do a Do. The self-imposed righteousness and the attempt to become an ideal person lead to inner conflict and can be quite stifling; it is the way of the ego and hence a destroyer. Freedom from it is not easy; it cannot come through any set of Dos and Don'ts. The growing inner awareness brings it along in its own way through making us a detached witness to ourselves.

When one listens to the Master, the non-verbal contact with the Inner Being is clear. It generates in us the ability to listen to the serene movement of life with the same detachment with which we listened to the Master's talk. If there is that quiet nonresistant contact with life, there is a natural order in one's behavior and Dos and Don'ts become unimportant. The natural order ensures such kindness and compassion that whatever the person does will be automatically right in the sense that it augments harmony and well-being in him and in others. No megalomania or fanaticism can find a place in one's mind under such conditions.

It is interesting to note the difference between the presentations of a moralizing preacher and an Enlightened Master.

The preachers usually speak from erudition and knowledge. They generally confine to the system to which they are emotionally attached and quote only from the scriptures belonging to that system. The talk centers on Dos and Don'ts and the associated moral codes. Such speakers expound prescribed paths, methods and techniques to reach predetermined, self-satisfying goals. Pious egoism plays a role. They seem to be unaware that all desires, whether for the worldly things or for the spiritual ones, arise from the same ego.

In contrast, the Masters speak from an inner transformation and direct awareness which is non-verbal knowingness. When they quote from scriptures, as they do occasionally, such scriptures span across several cultures and are not confined to any one system. Their talk generally moves outside of Dos and Don'ts, and contains only pointers for reflection and self-knowing. There is no insistence on conformity. The fact that all desires arise from the same state of mind is made clear; that is, the lust for heaven is no different from the lust for the woman, as mentioned earlier (Dikshit, 1973).

In some cases, however, the religious expositor (not exploiter!) may merely narrate religious or spiritual stories and not indulge in giving directives. Such discourses are different from the preaching type and may help in bringing about self-awareness. The expositor's talk can move the listener to be reflective and understand the hidden aspects of life.

The Practical Side versus the Inner Dive

Having said all that, we have to look at the flipside of the matter too. In handling practical matters of daily life, Dos and Don'ts are absolutely necessary. Without them, one is likely to be wayward, inefficient and unwise too. In contrast, when we turn inward and try to bring about a change with that approach, it becomes not only ineffective but can be counterproductive! Discretion is the watchword. A noninterfering, quiet self-awareness cannot come through any effort and that is why Dos and Don'ts are of no value there. A deep interest in that direction alone does the job. In fact, that interest itself is a result of self-awareness! Thus, the awareness and the interest it brings form a synergy. The conventional mind cannot grasp this because, according to it, any result must follow an effort; that is the effort and the result must be separated by time. Thus, the ego feeds on the illusion of forward moving time. Simultaneous existence of cause and effect cannot be perceived by the thought-ridden mind which forms the base of the ego. Again, it is a different matter in the practical world. There, cause and effect are separated by chronological time. When that concept enters the inner realm, psychological time is created, and it produces the 'I,' the cause of all trouble and unhappiness. While Dos and Don'ts are valued for running an efficient day-to-day life, their functioning in the inner realm is seen as a retarding force.

In chapter 5, we talked about several boxes to which people belong and their rigid confinement to those boxes. We also looked at the possibility of how people can free themselves from the slavery to such boxes. As long as human beings belong to one or more boxes, Dos and Don'ts hold strong sway on their psychology. Once there is a movement into the Esoteric Field, such directives lose their hold and the person breathes a sigh of relief. One feels as if a big weight has been taken away from one's shoulders. Those people, however, retain the wisdom of applying directives in the purely practical field.

Understanding resulting from self-awareness is a nonintellectual and passive movement; it is a movement away from the one guided by Dos and Don'ts. Change due to understanding oneself comes along imperceptibly and leads to fundamental transformation. This transformation cannot be influenced by any conditioning and is not along any preconceived notions. In contrast, change brought about by the conditioned mind is always limited in its content and will need never-ending corrections. It makes the waking hours of man enervating and exhausting by hitching him to a chase that has no end. Also, it leads to inner conflict and endless struggle. The accumulated knowledge in the mind interferes with everything and the noise prevents fundamental change from taking place. Fundamental change is at the neurological levels and, as mentioned before, cleanses centuries-old debris that man has inherited and bequeathed as a matter of biological continuance.

There are well-meaning books and articles such as "Five Steps towards Peace of Mind," "Ten ways to find Happiness," "Fifteen ways to becoming Rich," and the like. We do find in general that those books and articles are written by people with some insight into human ways. They give the reader a chance to apply oneself in order to bring about a turn in their lives towards betterment. Seriously-minded people have been helped by those books. However, such changes can only be peripheral and cannot touch the core of the being. Occasionally, they do bring about a lasting change in the individual because they touched something vital in the person's psychology. In general, though, the changes brought about by those Dos and Don'ts never last long and the individual will be back to square one sooner or later. This is because those steps are directed towards polishing the outer self and not towards understanding that self. Pure passivity is a state of humility in which there is no manipulation of oneself in order to reach a desired end. This detached bystander attitude is deeply cleansing and has the ability to bring about fundamental transformation. The dominance of 'I,' 'me' and the 'mine' begins to weaken. As mentioned before, the passivity does not come into being through the practice of any method. When one senses the beauty of its content, it flows in, like a gentle breeze, of its own accord.

The meaningfulness of passivity and the associated intrinsic transformation cannot be of value to the thought-ridden mind. While such a transformation furthers itself and becomes all comprehensive, no correction will ever be needed. The joy of being in the moment, being in the Now, establishes itself.

One cannot *decide* to be inwardly passive because the deciding to do something implies that one is being *active*, exactly the opposite! It leads us to the question, "Then, how on earth does passivity come into being?" The answer to this question is experiential, and so, non-verbal. To the one to whom that question becomes an intriguing puzzle, the Radial Dive sets in and brings up the answer from the depths of oneself. Everyone, without exception, has the answer to this puzzle in that infrequently visited region of one's Inner Being. As Masters often say, if one agrees to be guided from within, life becomes a venerable journey into the unknown.

In the Esoteric Field, importance is given as much to mundane matters as it is to the inner dive. As mentioned above, taking guidance from certain Dos and Don'ts helps us face daily life with some efficiency and wisdom. Here we see five of them. In the Esoteric Field, these manifest themselves in a natural way. Elsewhere too they are likely to make sense. An interesting question here is, "How is one to let them manifest in our lives without our having to struggle to bring them around?" That is a challenging question. Again, if we apply ourselves sincerely to them, we will discover the answer.

The Five Wise Items

The five items can be called nodal operations because each stands out from the other and demands to be applied with punch and precision. Those are given below. The reader can expand on these items or modify them to suit one's own temperament.

Delegate and Relegate: Sincere application to practical matters on hand setting apart proper attention and time to them, followed by unconcern, is what is implied in this. The approach can relieve the mind of unnecessary burden through thought-vortices. (The conventional use of the verb 'delegate' usually implies handing over duties or powers to somebody. Here, however, it is used in the sense of assigning time and attention to the matter on hand.)

Reflect and Reject: Items that emotionally disturb the mind deserve this kind of treatment. It involves calm reflection and understanding what requires to be done practically, followed by mental rejection of the issue. This prevents the mind from feeding on the item again and again as a matter of habit and negativity. The dog stops chasing its tail!

Accept and Act: It is good to accept people and things as they are and adapt oneself to them. This prevents rancor building up in us and helps us develop rapport with life, no matter what it chooses to bring. Soon this accepting and adapting oneself to life becomes a source of peace. Acceptance is to be followed by action to see how matters can be improved where necessary. A positive, constructive and optimistic approach is always healthy.

Love It and Leave It: Well-meaning aspirations (molded, fostered, kept clean and not sullied by thought) set up a healthy current in one's life. Such aspirations will be fulfilled on their own occasions. The usual problem is the psychological time that corrupts the mind. If we understand what it means to wait without knowing when, it will be a wonderful approach. In fact, there is then no waiting in the conventional sense of the word. This takes away the poison of psychological time. Once the aspirations are lovingly woven in a wholesome way in the interest of oneself and others, it is good to drop them into the bottomless abyss. They will sprout at the right time! We may even say, "Weave it and Leave it."

Henry David Thoreau (known as the Sage of the Walden Pond) is noted for his esoteric expositions. For a comprehensive collection of his writings, the reader is directed to the book *Walden and Other Writings* (Howarth, 1981). In connection with what we are looking for in these fourth of the five items, the following paragraph represents the essence of one of Thoreau's pointers.

If one respects one's aspirations and endeavors to conduct one's life in support of them, one will meet with a success well beyond the usual expectations. He will cross a tenuous boundary; universal and more liberal laws will begin to guide him as if he is given attention to by a higher order of beings. Life becomes progressively easier. One may think that one has only built castles in the air, but so long as the right foundation is put under them, the work need not be lost. The state of the future will depend on such application of ours in the 'Now'; mere passing of time cannot bring about that quality.

The tenuous boundary that Thoreau mentions can be likened to the Line of Transcendence in our Effervescence Model (chapter 5, Fig. 7). The above pointer of Thoreau has implications in both the mundane and esoteric matters. With regard to the latter, it may appear to be in contradiction with what we discussed in earlier chapters. We may ask: In what way is this matter of long-range aspirations different from getting embroiled in desires and greed? Won't it put forth time as future? It is good to reflect on this until each one finds the answer to this poser, allowing clarity to come up from one's inner realms. The difference is subtle but tangible to those who wish to strike a trail of their own.

Some aspirations may have to be revisited and rewoven. After having been at them for a while, there will be a natural detachment from them. It happens that, sooner or later, one disentangles oneself completely from those and stays floating; that is nothing weighs down heavily on the mind. There is a feeling that one has done all that is necessary to set in motion a healthy current. Detachment descends on one without the effort to be detached. This state of peacefulness makes one ripe for the next item.

Unconditionally Unload, Unfold and So Explode! Understanding this item requires self-awareness to the point of sensing how thought as habit accumulates poisonous garbage. Attention to this matter leads to unloading of all such garbage that would otherwise set up harmful offshoots in due course. Because of this unloading and the consequent clearing, Divine Essence unfolds from one's deeper region submerging one in a state of progressive calmness. It furthers itself, making our consciousness expand limitlessly. That is the explosion. So, it is a matter of implosion followed by explosion. In that respect, it resembles the stupendous astronomical phenomenon, the supernova!

The Outward and the Inward Riches

It is good to understand the outward riches as well as the inward riches of life on this planet. They are complementary to each other. In the Indian heritage, sixteen outer riches are recognized. They include good physical health and financial well-being too. The four stages of evolution of Jeevathma, the spark of the Divine in us, are given as Dharma, Artha, Kama and Moksha. They mean (1) virtuous conduct and behavior,

(2) wealth, (3) pleasures of life, and (4) Liberation. Unless the first three are gone through and transcended the right way, one doesn't become open to Liberation. It is interesting to note that in the age-old Tamil culture, the last item is indicated as 'Veedu,' meaning Home. That is, Liberation is actually a matter of returning home, the Divine spark rejoining the flame, as explained in chapter 6 under the caption Sankhya Philosophy. It is interesting to note that many Near Death Experience people talk about the feeling of returning home when they are on the other side.

Masters speak encouragingly about joyous things coming uninvited. "Resist not what comes uninvited" is their pointer. Ramana Maharishi too echoes this as part of his answers to questions. What may put up resistance to the good things coming uninvited is clearly the pious egoism, the tricky monster, mentioned earlier in chapter 7.

It is good to encourage the child to look into such topics as Astronomy, Anthropology, Archaeology and Paleontology; all these expand the cosmological awareness and help the child understand our little place in the vast scheme of things. Groupism and the associated fanaticism are less likely to control the child's psychology under those conditions. Treating others as one's honored co-passengers on the journey of life, regardless of what group they belong to, becomes a natural consequence to such an outlook. The child can then conduct its life in peace and harmony, and never become a party to jingoism, terrorism, violence and destruction.

Inward riches come through self-awareness and the associated inner dive. Abundant feeling and deep respect for everything and everyone are the primary characteristics of those riches. It is good to pay attention to both outward and inward riches. Every day becomes a significant day in one's life. There is no waiting for heaven or enlightenment that creates a psychological future. There is only applying oneself to the 'Now' wholeheartedly and letting the Consciousness at large, the mother of all things, take us wherever she will. That deep trust moves everything and makes us sense the loving presence of Divinity. God is not used any more as a utilitarian tool for salvation or ego-satisfaction. It becomes a matter of candid relationship with Divinity. Fear no longer plays a role in that link.

Chapter 13

Satori and Monism

Consciousness, the basis for our being aware of the world and the Universe, has many levels. These levels are characterized by different intensities of awareness. At a certain level, such as that in the animal, the intensity is not as much as in man. Among the animals themselves, there are various degrees of awareness. That is how the chimpanzee is able to respond better in terms of memory and interpretation than most other animals. The higher level of awareness in man has helped him understand nature's ways, harness nature's energies to his advantage and protect himself against many destructive forces. However, as of now, the awareness in the common man has not sufficiently evolved on this planet to transcend the ego. That is how even in the field of religion, ego plays a dominant role currently. From small family quarrels to war between nations, the basis for such unhappy situations is the ego; it is the thought-created entity characterized by limited awareness. An exception to this scenario is the state of Enlightenment in which awareness attains its fullness and the evolution of consciousness reaches its culmination. That state has been named variously as Satori, Liberation, Nirvana, Moksha, and Enlightenment. Satori is a Zen Buddhist term. Monism is a related word that comes to describe the state as an expansive consciousness in which the oneness of all is experienced (Advaita). There have been some human beings here and there throughout history, such as Krishna, Buddha, Jesus and Lao Tzu, in whom that state expressed itself. Evolution of consciousness puts up those flowers among human beings. However, the atmosphere is not yet strong enough to govern the general order of things through the deepening awareness and its holistic content. Ideas of self-importance, individual salvation and personal aggrandizement govern the psychology of the vast majority of people.

As awareness expands in a person, it makes him or her function from a background of love. Simultaneously, 'ahankara,' the source of egoistic approach to things, becomes weaker and weaker. Such people are a minority now because, for most human beings, the mind functions through identification with a nation, religion, race and the like. That is the approach by which the body-mind idea, one's individual name and form, gets crystallized as an image hardened by repetitive thought. This leads to separation and the associated defensive psychology. Deepening awareness takes the psychophysical system of a human being into vaster consciousness; that helps one get out of the individuation. Mind expands limitlessly dissolving the 'ahankara.' This is the beginning of Satori, the state of mind in which the universal oneness is felt and the fundamental truth understood. The Upanishads say that when one sees himself in all creatures and all creatures in himself, he is said to have crossed the ocean of sorrow.

The phenomenon of rainbow serves as an analogy. A rainbow does not exist as a separate object in the sky. In other words, if there is no onlooker there is no rainbow. It is an occurrence that clearly includes the observer as an integral part of the phenomenon. Thus, with deeper perspective, it becomes clear that there is no experience without the experiencer. They form an inseparable unit. This awareness can help us understand the basic substratum on which everything stands.

Satori literally means 'to understand.' We gather something about it from what the Masters tell us. It is a matter of understanding the Ultimate, not as a matter of knower and the known, but by being the Ultimate. In other words, there is dissolution of all divisions. The duality as the perceiver and the perceived ceases and the two merge in a state of oneness, as a state of perception. That state is totally different from the conventional perception in which the separation between the knower and the known appears real. Adi Sankara talks about Sakhshi Chaitanyam, a witness consciousness that is aware of everything and itself.

Deepening self-awareness brings the spiritually inclined person to the brink of receiving the Ultimate. Initially, Satori visits that person sporadically because the mind has not yet developed the ability to sustain that state. Such experiences are known as Kensho in the Zen terminology. It signals the first perception of the Buddha-Nature. The Kensho experience comes and goes. Satori, on the other hand, refers to a stable state of unity with the cosmos. It is similar to the developments in a baby. The baby tries to stand upright; holds itself in balance; walks a few steps and falls; after repeated such events, the baby becomes confident in walking. In the ancient Sanskrit texts, Kensho and Satori are referred to as Kevala Samadhi and Sahaja Samadhi respectively.

Appendices 1, 2 and 3 give accounts by three human beings who experienced Satori for brief spells; they went through Kensho. (In this book, the name Satori is used as a generic term.) This chapter on Satori and Monism would be incomplete without reference to the appendices. Anyone who is drawn to the Esoteric Field would be deeply stirred by those accounts. Under Satori, one gets an intense experience of the all-pervading Divinity, an actuality beyond all mental concepts of God and the associated religious definitions. One also perceives the myth behind psychological time and therefore directly senses the truth behind timelessness. Unimaginable silence pervades the consciousness.

When the mind is caught in vortices of thought, such as those due to fear, anger, attachment and the like, it becomes so noisy it cannot be receptive to the universal energy and the universal intelligence that support the whole cosmos. The mind bruised by the scratching effects of suffering lacks the freshness and the ability to receive the immensity. When through self-awareness the harmful vortices (fear, anger, regret and the like) slow down, the mind begins to sense the beauty of the cosmic oneness and allows itself to be a receptacle to the inflow. Sooner or later, it is flooded with Satori.

What energizes the vortices is the threefold attachment, attachment to people, things and ideas. This attachment cannot be forcibly driven away because such an effort itself shows attachment to the ideal of detachment! It is such a tricky trap that the mind falls victim to it by its own proclivity. That is how people, though well-meaning in their religious and spiritual practices, succumb to attachments: Attachments to gurus, scriptures, theology, concepts, and practices. Freedom from attachments is not easy because it does not result from effortful action. Those in the Esoteric Field realize this and keep wondering as to how this freedom comes into being at all. This wonderment is a facet of self-awareness that frees one from effortful actions and, hence, to a relaxed state of mind. This augments the inner dive that works its way silently towards the Inner Being. The mind becomes open to cataclysmic changes, and so to Satori. Movement into the loving field of Divinity takes place of its own accord because the obstacles are removed. This movement is pure in the sense that it is free of all self-interest and is untouched by cultural and religious conditioning.

Kurt Friedrichs (Appendix 3) mentions that the Satori experiences, which visited him repeatedly on the little island of Heligoland in the North Sea, had the important characteristic that they did not arise as a result of his power or volition; rather, they rushed at him without his control, always leaving behind an indescribable happiness. The ultimate oneness arising out of union with the cosmos is clear from the expression of Kurt Friedrichs.

In general, three stages can be recognized in the movement towards the Monistic (Advaitic) state of mind. The first: One is drawn to spiritual matters but is not free from the 'I am the body' idea. Even if he may say that he is not the body, he is still identified with the mind-made image of himself. The second: Freedom from the body-mind idea begins to establish itself; Kensho can take place here. The third: Well-established in the knowledge of Universal Oneness (Satori).

The idea of eternal heaven is time based and so it is mind-sponsored within the realm of the ego. During Satori, the illusion of time is perceived; with that perception, all items associated with time disappear. Those whose minds expand into the Universal Consciousness understand the actuality of timelessness; they find it hard to give expression to it within the intelligibility of the conventional mind.

People who go through a near death experience often report sensing the same silence, the timelessness, the universal oneness and the abundant compassion with which it floods them. Victor Solow gives an account of what he experienced when he had a cardiac arrest and was clinically dead for about 20 minutes (Solow, 1974). He says that, even after several years past that experience, a nostalgic memory remains for the other reality, that state of indescribable stillness and quiet where the 'I' is part of a harmonious whole. That peace cannot be experienced while still being identified as a separate entity. Thus, one cannot know that state of Satori by any stretch of imagination, but only by being directly absorbed in it. Those who have been into it report that the feeling of being a separate individual is dissolved in the Universal Consciousness. The illusion of being a separate entity vanishes.

Advaita means a non-dual state; it is in that state that the usual dualistic feeling arising out of the 'I here, God there' attitude is seen to be an illusion. That is why it is called a Monistic state. Nothing apart from Divinity exists. All else is merely a phantasmagoria, a shadow created by the mind because of its limited awareness. Here, a quote from Meister Eckhart would be relevant: "The knower and the known are one. Simple people imagine that they should see God as if He stood there and they here. This is not so. God and I, we are one in knowledge."

In the Advaitic state, awareness reaches its fullness and the illusion of duality is cleared. Monism transcends Monotheism because the latter involves the 'I here, God there' dualism. 'Unity in Diversity' is experienced in Advaita as the fundamental Truth. In the ancient writings of Indian heritage there is a related statement: "The Absolute is one but sages refer to it diversely." In chapter 8, we touched upon the matter of Radical Transformation. Such a transformation precedes the Advaitic state.

The bliss of ego-free state cannot be bought through any sacrifice, virtue or drug as it is not a reward. Whatever is produced as a secondary thing (upadhi, in Sanskrit) is related to the Entity molded by thought; when that mold disappears, the 'other,' the Primary Essence which has always been there, rushes in. The 'other' has no beginning and no end, and so everything is a subset to it. That is how an 'upadhi' cannot produce it. Obviously, a part cannot produce the whole any more than a child can produce its mother!

An article by Dr. Suzuki appeared in the *Mountain Path*, a journal of Ramanasramam, in the year 1995 under the title "The Meaning of Satori" (Suzuki, 1995). In it, he brings out clearly several aspects of the Monistic state. The following paragraphs are taken from that article:

When you try to realize Satori, the more you struggle, the farther away it is. You cannot help pursuing Satori, but so long as you make that special effort, Satori will never be gained. But you cannot forget about it altogether. If you expect Satori to come to you of its own accord, you will not get it.

To realize Satori is very difficult, as the Buddha found. When he wished to be liberated from the bondage of birth and death he began to study philosophy, but this did not avail him, so he returned to asceticism. This made him so weak that he could not move, so he took milk and decided to go on with his search for liberation. Reasoning did not do any good and pursuing moral perfection did not help him either. Yet the urge to solve this problem was still there. He could not go any farther, yet he could not retreat, so he had to stay where he was, but even that would not do. This state of spiritual crisis means that you cannot go on, nor retreat, nor stay where you are. When this dilemma is genuine, there prevails a state of consciousness ready for Satori. When we really come to this stage, when we find ourselves in the critical moment, something is sure to rise from the depths of reality, from the depths of our own being. When this comes up, there is Satori. Then you understand all things and are at peace with the world as well as with yourself.

Going through the above lines of Dr. Suzuki, we see that the transformation leading to Satori is indeed enigmatic. That is what makes it so interesting. If we understand the fact that our exerting effort cannot help, it does make us feel at ease; however, the pull towards it does not leave us free! What is one to do when whatever one does becomes a movement away from the Truth? The mind feels completely stumped, gives up and remains quiet. That provides the right grounds for Satori to take place.

Chapter 14

Epilogue

It is said in Chinese philosophy that a good traveler never arrives. In this journey of life, the participant goes on taking part in the travel while also progressively detaching oneself from it inwardly. One is both on it and not on it. Thus, the traveler never arrives! It is a paradox and the wider consciousness can say something about it. Therein lies the beauty of the journey of life. It is more a matter of changing circumstances rather than one of movement in time.

We have been co-passengers so far in the journey through the book and have now come to its last phase. During the journey, we touched upon several issues related to daily life with a slant on the Radial Dive and the movement towards the Deeper Self. When we become interested in the cosmological significance of our existence, life moves us on to the joy of discovery. Otherwise, our minds circle within a limited cocoon dominated by ego-based self-centered activities.

The Esoteric Field, introduced as the main idea in this book, is not a field isolated from the mundane life. It is a comprehensive zone in which the mundane life is a subset. When a subset tries to usurp the place of the whole, there is disharmony and unhappiness. Once we become aware of this, the mundane life takes its rightful place and all is well.

As a child grows up in the present world, the atmosphere is one of success worship, success in the matters here or in the hereafter. Education does not give much importance to the cosmological significance of life and the child is lost in the thicket of competition and self-importance. The difference between self-care and selfishness is not made clear to the child.

The aim of this book has been to draw the attention of the reader to the relatively less explored areas of living that can add richness to our lives, richness in a comprehensive sense of the word. The associated expansive awareness is a matter of joy. The word richness here includes financial well-being too, but it will come up in wholesome and harmonious ways; not through cutthroat competitions, by stepping on others' toes or similar selfish ways. In the Esoteric Field, barriers due to nationality, religion, language and the like disappear. There is no groupism. Aloneness and its purity shine forth.

The Immensity

The vastness of the universe, in space and time, is a measure of its immensity, not only in physical measures but also in terms of its esoteric content. That content of intelligence and energy holds everything together in a continuum of order and harmony. There are no chance happenings. When we remember this as we go about our daily chores, our minds develop wide elbowroom. The freedom arising out of it helps us conduct our life with sublime austerity.

Hubert Reeves takes us on a picnic through the universe with his book *Atoms of Silence* (Reeves, 1984). He talks about a Kalpa in the tradition of India which is the periodicity with which the universe functions in its cyclic process of birth, life and death. He goes on to give an interesting anecdote of how the Buddha described the duration of a Kalpa in a story. Every once in a hundred years an old man comes along to polish a mountain that is bigger than the Himalayas, with a handkerchief made of the fine Benares silk. After one Kalpa, the mountain would have been worn down to the sea!

Hubert says that he amused himself with an approximate calculation of the duration for a Kalpa based on the above metaphor. He found that the time required is entirely compatible with the 10^{32} years (100,000,000,000,000,000,000,000,000,000,000 years) calculated by scientists as a measure of the cyclic period sustained by the Universe.

Astronomy is one of the fields that remind us of the immensity around us. Wikipedia says that Voyager 1, already the most distant man-made object in the cosmos, reached 100 astronomical units from the sun on August 15, 2006. That means the spacecraft, launched nearly four decades ago, will be 100 times more distant from the Sun than the Earth is.

Let us look at another example from our space age, the one of Voyager II. It was a spacecraft sent by the United States in 1977 to study some planets in the solar system. After passing close to the intended planets, the craft left the solar system at a speed of about 56,000 km per hour (approximately 35,000 mi/hour). That is an unimaginable speed. It is equivalent to about 15 km/sec (9 mi/sec). If you are standing (a little away from its path, of course!) hoping to see it, Woosh, it is gone! You can't see it. It is too fast and before you know it is coming, it is gone. A tremendous feat by a group of scientists and engineers!

Voyager II is traveling in a curvilinear path because of the complex motion influenced by the rotation and gravity of the Earth and the solar system. If it were to go in a straight-line path to Sirius, one of our nearby stars, it would take 190,000 years to reach the star! Can one imagine that mind-boggling distance between us and Sirius? If that were so for a nearby star, what to speak of those distant stars and the even more distant galaxies? An unimaginable magnitude of void exists between those celestial objects. If we watch the stellar canopy on a clear night, the awesome depth of the Universe makes a profound impact on us. We get an inkling of the immensity in which we live.

Man in his present anatomy and physiology is reported to have lived on this planet for one and a half million years or so. In contrast, those huge dinosaurs of gargantuan proportions roamed the Earth for 160 million years! (That number keeps changing to higher values!) They passed away only recently, just 65 million years ago. There are other similar facts that take us for a ride across the immensity of the Universe, immensity in space and time. Scientists have double checked and triple checked those numbers and so, for sure, they do not take us for a ride! Compared to those staggering dimensions, we seem to be totally insignificant. But not quite so! Because those immensities, colossal as they may be, are still perceived by the mind functioning in the little human brain. The Masters say that when the mind is free and liberated, it enters the Consciousness that fills the whole Universe! Reflections on these help us feel the intriguing nature of the Universe and Divinity.

Victor Solow (Solow, 1974) says, after his NDE, that this wonderful world of light and shadows, children, flowers and lovers, this deadly place of evil and suffering, is only one of many realities through which we must travel to distant and unknown destinations. Belonging to this world is one rung in many on the ladder towards the ultimate Reality. However, the Masters say that one can jump off from any rung on the ladder to that Reality. The merely rational mind may not be impressed by these esoteric statements.

Some Shakespearean lines give a supportive drumming to the above aspect: *There are more things in heaven and earth, Horatio, than are dreamt of in your philosophy.* To ignore all those cosmological immensities and to let one's life be guided merely by thoughts of personal salvation can only be considered a deplorable degradation.

As mentioned in chapter 9, the other intriguing feature is the long journey of the soul across many incarnate and discarnate periods through which the Entity around a soul evolves. It is to be noted that, according to that process, all souls cleanse themselves and return Home and there is no such thing as eternal damnation for any entity.

The Comprehensive Care

The individual evolution is also linked to the evolution of collective consciousness on the planet. In this connection, the book *Conscious Evolution* by Barry McWaters makes for interesting reading (McWaters, 1983). Its subtitle is: Personal and Planetary Transformation.

Sir George Trevelyan's preface to that book contains a spirited appeal to all of us towards taking part in the evolution of consciousness on this planet. He says that in a dramatic way, present scientific advancements are rediscovering the great truths known to the ancient mystery traditions of the West and, of course, to Oriental wisdom. He adds that we should see the history of Earth as a story of the evolution of consciousness. His emphasis is on the fact that the spearhead of evolution now turns inwards into the individual. Each one of us is offered the opportunity of taking conscious direction and control of oneself so that we become the stewards of the planet.

Sir George Trevelyan is convinced that the energies of transformation are now being flooded into our planet and that an operation for revitalizing the planet has been launched from the cosmological intelligence. He points out that what Barry McWaters brings up in his book is not merely an intellectual plan for improving society but a vision of the human task and challenge for redeeming the planet. We should become aware of the great opportunity offered to us at the threshold of the Aquarian Epoch to participate in the evolution of Universal Consciousness here on the Earth. There is no doubt that to be born as a human being on this blue marble in space at the present period provides an intriguing as well as an exciting scenario. Those who feel drawn to the Esoteric Field are sure to have a deep chord struck in them by what Sir George Trevelyan has put forth. For them, the book by McWaters can be quite inspiring.

The Masters tell us that when we direct our attention inward, what we are doing is a contribution to the profound transformation that is taking place in the collective consciousness of man, perhaps beyond the planet too! It is a waking up of consciousness from mistaken identification with form and the resulting individuation. We are stepping out of the rut into which human beings have fallen for untold centuries. The silent energy that goes forth from a person, whose mind is quiet due to self-awareness, is potent and tends to harmonize conflicting forces to produce a world of happiness and peace. One Master (Tolle, 2003) makes our spirits buoyant by saying that positive forces are already at work on this planet; it is not so apparent because the negative forces are making a louder noise. That should give us enough encouragement. We cooperate.

There is openness in the psychology of a person who shows interest in understanding the deeper issues of life, body and mind. With that openness, one becomes a channel for higher energies to descend on humanity. You may remain unknown to the public and media because there will be no hankering after social fame on your part. One understands that basking under the social image can create obstruction to self-awareness and the inner dive.

There are those who have developed attachment to some prophesies and believe that the world is doomed to come to an end soon. They seem to like the idea. If you are not one among them, you can help produce a transformation in the collective consciousness towards bringing about a world of happy and caring human beings. That situation can also prevent the impending environmental doom.

Treating each day as an honored element of life on this planet brings about a wholesome joy. It enriches one's individual life while also giving momentum to the evolution of consciousness on Earth. The journey of life becomes venerable and it reflects in the sacredness of our relationships. What triggers interest in that direction is the serious questioning of accepted norms created by conventional approaches and sectarian religious practices. We went through some items in the earlier chapters that can act as catalysts to free us from that syndrome.

Years ago, a despondent Oliver Goldsmith wrote, *"Harken, O Posterity, to thee I call!"* Alright, we are not despondent. Nevertheless, we take the cue from Oliver and blow the trumpet to say, *"Harken, O Reader of these lines, to thee we call!"* Call for what? It is a call to indulge in the fun of self-awareness and to bring about a transformation towards self-discovery and the discovery of Divinity. In the process, we would have participated in the permeation of Universal Consciousness on this planet. We wouldn't be thinking of using the Supreme to our own selfish ends. When we pay attention to the larger purpose, our own little corner is enriched too. Transformation in collective consciousness takes place only when it takes place in the individual; indeed, the two are simultaneous. Thus, attention to the Esoteric Field elevates both the individual and the whole of humanity at the same time.

We have now come to the end of our journey through the book. Our journey of life, however, continues. Perhaps we will be fellow passengers again!

In the Indian heritage, all ceremonies end with a fervent cosmopolitan prayer that means, "May all people of the world be happy and well." We end the journey through the book with the same line:

Lokah samasta sukhino bhavanthu.

Author Biography

Gopalakrishnan TC was born in Chennai, India, in 1941; graduated in 1963 in Civil Engineering from the Engineering College, Madras University. Received the Master's degree from the Indian Institute of Technology, Madras, while being on the teaching and research faculty there in the Hydraulic Engineering Department. His doctoral degree was in the field of Coastal Engineering from the North Carolina State University, Raleigh, NC, USA in 1978. Served as Assistant Professor in that university for two years and then worked as a Research Scientist at the Kuwait Institute for Scientific Research for eight years. Presented technical papers on coastal engineering in international conferences held in USA, England, Belgium, Switzerland, Japan, Australia and China.

Aside from his professional involvements, he was interested in the philosophic aspects of life on this planet. This led him to the messages of the great masters like Lao Tzu, Buddha, Jesus Christ, Ramana Maharishi and J. Krishnamurti. His book *In Quest of the Deeper Self*, self-published in 2007, is the outcome of his reflections on those and his wish to share the outcome with others. The current book *The Journey into Oneself* is a revised form of that book.

Gopalakrishnan has been a member of the International Association for Near Death Studies, Durham, NC, USA. He presented a paper at their International Conference held in Durham, NC, USA, in September 2011; the title of the paper: *The Spiritual Content of Near Death Experiences*.

Gopalakrishnan lives in Kodaikanal, a hill town in South India, with his wife Banumathy. They have a daughter and son who are both married and settled.

Appendix 1

An Experience of Satori

The contents for this appendix and the next are excerpted from the interviews that two gentlemen had with Krishnaji (as J. Krishnamurti was affectionately called by his close associates). That was sometime in the middle part of the twentieth century. The interviews appeared in a publication titled *Commentaries on Living: Second Series*, edited by D. Rajagopal and published by Krishnamurti Foundation of India (Rajagopal, 1991). The excerpts given here provide a glimpse of the expansion of consciousness. However, it is recommended that the reader take recourse to the above reference to enjoy the impact of the full interview. This appendix is from the article, "Cleansed of the Past," on page 171 of the book cited.

Appendices 1 and 2 primarily represent presentations by two gentlemen who experienced Satori as a ravishing experience while moving along their normal life. There are some similarities in their presentations which give us a glimpse of the Universal Consciousness; what stand out are (1) sensing the Beyond, and (2) the oneness of all creation. As is the wont in all articles of the above-referenced book, Krishnaji describes the natural surroundings in which he finds himself around the time and place of the interviews. That part of the two articles is not given here. Further, Krishnaji's response to the two men's queries at the end of their presentations is also not included. Readers are directed to the original article for his response. The objective of the two appendices here is only to highlight the elements of a Satori experience.

Grateful thanks are due to the Krishnamurti Foundation for giving permission to reproduce the relevant paragraphs here.

The gentleman who meets Krishnaji in the article "Cleansed of the Past" happens to be a painter who passed through very difficult times through the two world wars; during the second war, he lost his family members. He gives a brief outline of his biography to Krishnaji and then narrates his experience in the following lines:

"I am telling you all this not to just ramble on about myself, but to give you a sketch of my background, for in talking things over with you I may get to understand something which has become very vital to me. Nothing else interests me, not even my painting.

One day I set out for those hills with my painting things, for I had seen something over there which I wanted to paint. It was fairly early in the morning when I got to the place, and there were a few clouds in the sky. From where I was I could see across the valley to the bright sea. I was enchanted to be alone, and I began to paint. I must have been painting for some time, and it was coming along beautifully, without any strain or effort, when I became aware that something was taking place inside my head, if I could put it that way. I was so absorbed in my painting that for a while I did not notice what was happening to me, and then suddenly I was aware of it. I could not go on with my painting, but I sat very still."

After a moment's pause, the gentleman continues.

"Don't think me crazy, for I am not, but sitting there I was aware of an extraordinarily creative energy. It wasn't I that was creative, but something in me, something that was also in those ants and in that restless squirrel. I don't think I am explaining this very well, but surely you understand what I mean. It was not the creativeness of some Tom, Dick or Harry writing a poem or of myself painting a silly picture; it was just creation, pure and simple, and the things produced by the mind or by the hand were on the outer fringes of this creation, with little significance. I seemed to be bathed in it; there was a sacredness about it, a benediction. If I were to put it in religious words, I would say... but I won't. Those religious words stick in my mouth; they no longer have any meaning. It was the center of Creation, God himself... Again, these words! But I tell you, it was holy, not the man made holiness of churches, incense and hymns, which is all immature nonsense. This was something uncontaminated, unthought-of, and tears were rolling down my cheeks; I was being cleansed of all my past. The squirrel had stopped fretting about its next meal, and there was an astonishing silence, not the silence of the night when all things sleep, but a silence in which everything was awake.

I must have sat there, motionless, for a very long time, for the sun was in the west; I was a little stiff, one leg had gone to sleep, and I could stand up only with difficulty, I am not exaggerating, Sir, but time seemed to have stopped, or rather, there was no time. I had no watch, but several hours must have passed from the moment I put my brush down to the moment I got up. I was not hysterical, nor had I been unconscious, as some might conclude; on the contrary, I was fully alert, aware of everything that was happening around me. Picking up all my things and carefully putting them in my knapsack, I left, and in that extraordinary state walked back to my house. All the noises of a small town did not in any way disturb that state, and it lasted for several hours after I got home. When I awoke the next morning, it was completely gone. I looked at my painting; it was good, but nothing outstanding."

The above lines usually touch a deep chord in us. It is good to resonate with it and then leave it alone. A background serenity would keep us company.

Appendix 2

Yet Another Satori

Here we give an account by a second person who meets Krishnaji regarding an experience similar to the one described in Appendix 1. This is taken from the article, "An Experience of Bliss," on page 151 of *Commentaries on Living: Second Series* (Rajagopal, 1991).

The person who meets Krishnaji on this occasion is a successful businessman. He gives a graphic account of the state of mind under Satori. Similar to the account in Appendix 1, the three items that stand out in this Satori are: (1) the astonishing silence, (2) the oneness of all, and (3) the truth about timelessness. He tells Krishnaji that he had a most remarkable experience which completely ravished his heart and that, though he had read of those things, they were always empty words and appealed only to his senses. He says that what happened to him was beyond all thought, beyond imagination and desire.

Now we listen to his actual words:

I woke up one morning very early; the city was still asleep and its murmur had not yet begun. I felt I had to get out, so I dressed quickly and went down the street. Even the milk truck was not yet on its rounds. It was early spring and the sky was pale blue. I had a strong feeling that I should go to the park, a mile or so away. From the moment I came out of my front door I had a strange feeling of lightness, as though I were walking on air. The building opposite, a drab block of flats, had lost all its ugliness; the very bricks were alive and clear. Every little object which ordinarily I would not have noticed seemed to have an extraordinary quality of its own, and strangely, everything seemed to be a part of me. Nothing was separate from me; in fact, the 'me' as the observer, was absent, if you know what I mean. There was no me separate from that tree, or from that paper in that gutter, or from the birds that were calling to each other. It was a state of consciousness that I had never known.

On the way to the park, there is a flower shop. I have passed it hundreds of times, and I used to glance at the flowers as I went by. But on this particular morning I stopped in front of it. The plate glass window was slightly frosted with the heat and damp from inside, but this did not prevent me from seeing the many varieties of flowers. As I stood looking at them, I found myself smiling and laughing with a joy I had never before experienced. Those flowers were speaking to me, and I was speaking to them; I was among them and they were part of me. In saying this, I may give you the impression that I was hysterical, slightly off my head; but it was not so. I had dressed very carefully, and had been aware of putting on clean things, looking at my watch, seeing the names of the shops, including that of my tailor, and reading the titles of the books in a bookshop window. Everything was alive and I loved everything. I was the scent of those flowers, but there was no 'me' to smell the flowers, if you know what I mean. There was no separation between them and me. That flower shop was fantastically alive with colors, and the beauty of it all must have been stunning, for time and its measurement had ceased. I must have stood there for over twenty minutes, but I assure you there was no sense of time. I could hardly tear myself away from those flowers. The world of struggle, pain and sorrow was there and yet it was not. You see, in that state words have no meaning. Words are descriptive, separative, comparative, but in that state, there were no words; 'I' was not experiencing, there was only that state, that experience. Time had stopped; there was no past, present or future. There was only, oh, I don't know how to put into words, but it doesn't matter. There was a Presence; no, not that word. It was as though the earth, with everything in it and on it, was in a state of benediction, and I, walking towards the park, was part of it. As I drew near the park I was absolutely spellbound by the beauty of those familiar trees. From the pale yellow to the black green, the leaves were dancing with life; every leaf stood out separate, and the whole richness of the earth was in a single leaf. I was conscious that my heart was beating fast; I have a very good heart, but I could hardly breathe as I entered the park, and I thought I was going to faint. I sat down on a bench, and tears were rolling down my cheeks. There was a silence that was utterly unbelievable, but that silence was cleansing all things of pain and sorrow. As I went deeper into the park, there was music in the air. I was surprised, as there was no house nearby, and no one would have a radio at that hour of the morning. The music was part of the whole thing. All the goodness, all the compassion of the world was in that park, and God was there.

I am not a theologian, nor much of a religious person. I have been a dozen times or so inside a church, but it has never meant anything to me. I cannot stomach all that nonsense that goes on in churches. But in that park, there was a Being, if one may use such a word, in whom all things lived and had their being. My legs were shaking, and I was forced to sit down again, with my back against a tree. The trunk was a living thing, as I was, and I was part of that tree, part of that Being, part of the world. I must have fainted. It had all been too much for me; the vivid, living colors, the leaves, the rocks, the flowers, and the incredible beauty of everything. And over all was the benediction of...

When I came to, the sun was up. It generally takes me about twenty minutes to walk to the park, but it was nearly two hours since I left my house. Physically I seemed to have no strength to walk back; so, I sat there, gathering strength and not daring to think. As I slowly walked back home, the whole of that experience was with me; it lasted two days and faded away as suddenly as it had come. Then my torture began. I didn't go near my office for a week. I wanted that strange living experience back again. I wanted to live once again and forever in that beatific world. All this happened two years ago. I have seriously thought of giving up everything and going away into some lonely corner of the world, but I know in my heart that I cannot get it back that way. No monastery can offer me that experience, nor can any candle-lit church, which only deals with death and darkness. I considered making my way to India, but that too I put aside. Then I tried a certain drug; it made things more vivid, and so on, but an opiate is not what I want. That is a cheap way of experiencing; it is a trick but not the real thing.

Appendix 3

The Universal Consciousness

John Yale edited and published a book titled *What Vedanta Means to Me* containing seminar presentations by Westerners who had studied the Indian spiritual text Vedanta (Yale, 1955). One of those speakers is Kurt Friedrichs. Given below is an excerpt from his presentation. Grateful thanks are due to the Vedanta Press, a unit of Vedanta Society of Southern California, for granting permission to reproduce here some paragraphs from that essay. Kurt had studied several esoteric publications from both the East and the West. In his presentation given below, he describes his own experience of moving into the Universal Consciousness and his reflections on the esoteric literature.

On the little island of Heligoland in the North Sea, where I first became conscious of the phenomenal world around me, there were only a few objects between the sky and the sea to which one might have become attached; and the few space filling things were heavy, mighty, and at first seemed to me to be fortunately unalterable.

My youth among the red rocks on the island was made up of books and solitude and permitted a mysterious imaginative capacity to grow up within me, which made me completely independent of my environment and people. As there was nobody in my shut off world with whom I could have shared my strange experiences, let alone a teacher with a trained intellect or a spiritual leader. The relationships and connections with my own self remained hidden to me for many years, although the experiences themselves were none the less intense and impressive. They had only the important difference that they did not arise as a result of my own power and volition but rather rushed at me without control, and always left an indescribable happiness behind them.

From my earliest youth I was governed by a strange, ungrounded fear, fear of each morning to come, of every meeting with people; each new day seemed to be filled with threatening unrest, insecurity and uncertainty. Sadness and melancholy often occupied my thoughts to such an extent that in tiredness and resignation I yearned for a never ending sleep from which there would be no return to this horrible world. But one day there came an experience which soon in the force of its repetition was to become much finer and more sublime than the deepest and longest sleep could be.

One afternoon at low tide on the west coast of the island, as I was climbing over the seaweed-covered rocks in order to have a rest beneath an overhanging cliff, washed out by the surf of many centuries, a spiritual ecstasy suddenly took possession of me. The waves breaking at my feet and the endless surface of water stretching away to the vanishing point all of a sudden threw me into another sphere of consciousness. I myself was surf, sea and infinity. Time, space, body-consciousness, everything was blotted out, drawn up into an absolute consciousness of light and bliss. I have no idea of how long this condition lasted, but I felt the elation long afterwards until it slowly made room again for the fear that this experience, as an arbitrary condition brought about by chance, would never recur, and my state of mind might be worse than before in its insatiable longing for complete unity with the whole world.

And yet beneath the same cliff wall, in the rhythm of breaking waves and the swinging harmony of the endless sky and sea, I was again and again thrown out of rational and bodily limitations. But however much my normal consciousness searched and rationalized, it could not explain this condition of transformation, and I sought yearningly for descriptions of similar experiences in the writings of the great humanity who bear witness to the tireless struggle for knowledge and truth.

I found wonderful descriptions of contemplation in the works of such mystics as Eckhart, Suso, Tauler, Ruysbroeck, and Boehme. Their God vision was to me the expression of the highest experience of divine ecstasy. With fanatic zeal I read everything I could discover on metaphysics, philosophy, psychology, mysticism and religion. Everywhere the same truths, differentiated only by degree! What an incomparable rational experience, to find accounts of the same truth in Pythagoras, in Plato, in the Eleusinian Mysteries, in the experience of the Buddhist saints, in Zen, in the Tao Te Ching, in the Upanishads, and in the Gita. After all these truths from the various centuries, recognized by various races of various confessions, the saying of the Vedas seems to soothe and encourage: 'Truth is one, but sages call it by various names.'

While studying Buddhism I received for the first time the certainty that every man is destined to attain liberation as soon as he is willing to pay the price for it, namely, giving up all his attachments. And once, after long considering such thoughts, it seemed as if I was once again sitting under that cliff at home. Before me lay the ocean of world-consciousness; all sects, all religions, all struggles for truth; waves of the same ocean. So many spiritually striving people, so many great and small waves, so many ways to God.

Soon afterwards I entered the gigantic thought construction of the Vedanta, this genius work created by the eternal human search for truth. From the Advaita Vedanta of Adi Sankara that same bliss flowed upon me which I had experienced as a child viewing the endless sea. In amazement I learned that all worry, all fear, was vain; that my human birth and the irresistible yearning for liberation had set me on the way to the final goal. Vedanta gave me the certainty that every seeker obtains help from the great souls who have already traveled along that path and to whom all-embracing knowledge brought also all-embracing love. Vedanta magically transformed the world for me. I suddenly saw the phenomenal world in a completely different light, and behind the material universe the eternal principles dawned upon me. It soon seemed to me a matter of course that every spiritually-minded person was destined to meet Vedanta, because each bears Vedanta in himself and can experience the highest state only in the final identification of Atman and Brahman.

When Europe became involved in war, which tore me away from my beloved island, I got to know the cities of the Continent as well, with their masses and the dreadful turmoil of secularized civilization; a devouring longing for the experiences beside the sea took possession of me. I yearned for nothing other than island solitude and the extension of my previous experiences to the complete penetration of myself.

But the war took everything, even my home, with all the earthly possessions that men call their own. And even for years afterwards bombs burst upon the cliffs of my native land, tearing up the graves of my forefathers. Without Vedanta I would have become the victim of despair, grief and hate. But its knowledge brought me piece of mind. It taught me that, even home and the nearest and dearest of my conceptions and memories, had to break down so that I might become free from all attachments in order to attain the truth that there is only one enduring home, only one refuge in the universe: the Self. And I experienced the same as Omar Khayyam who searching for the Dschemshid's bowl that mirrored the world, learned from his master that he himself was the famous goblet. But this time it was not to stop at mere rational knowledge; this time the teacher was found who knew the way to realization and the price which had to be paid. Through study of the scriptures, company of enlightened souls, japam and meditation, Vedanta proved to me that the wonderful extension of consciousness towards an all embracing oneness, which I had enjoyed as a grace on the island, was my own birthright, my own Self, my real, divine nature. Vedanta showed me that, after overcoming all causal limitations, it was possible to become absolute consciousness.

Today Vedanta is no longer a mere dry, intellectual construction for me, no abstract conception; rather it is the highest wisdom of my own Self, an all-embracing expression for all human striving towards truth and light.

What a man once knows he can never forget. And if one knows Vedanta to be the way to the knowledge of the Self, then one reaches the light, just as a cave acquires light when a candle is lit, even if it has lain in darkness for centuries.

Appendix 4

The Hidden Harmony

Beyond hope, belief and faith, there is the field of Trust. Where there is Trust, there is intrinsic goodness. Born in the stillness of one's Deeper being, it spills over and permeates one's outer consciousness. It has nothing to do with religious sentimentalism and beliefs. This Trust is not placed in someone or in a system but in the very movement of life. With this Trust, the mundane and esoteric responsibilities are fulfilled with ease. Abundant feelings and deep respect flow towards everyone and everything, like a primordial fountain.

Beyond even the field of Trust is the zone of Knowingness, the very abode of the Ultimate, of the pervasive Divinity. Paradoxically, this zone is not somewhere 'out there' but deep within oneself, and curiously, once entered it fills the whole Universe! Whether one knows it or not, our journey of life on this planet is taking each one of us to that zone sedulously, through its joyous and happy days, its trials and tribulations. No one is condemned. Like a mother walking in a busy marketplace extending her hand for the child to hold, the journey of life bestows its care upon us. Our job is to cooperate with it, be seasoned by its sorrows, elevated by its joys and tickled by its fun. This helps us chime in with the journey and move towards an ever deepening harmony. In the process, the loving presence of Divinity is felt, beyond all religious concepts and ideas of personal salvation. With deep trust in its motherly care, let us enjoy the ride and be a dispassionate witness to the Divine Drama.

...Gopalakrishnan TC

References

Aiken, A. (1997) *That Which Is*. Birmingham: Hillier Press.

Atwater, P.M.H. (1989) *Coming Back to Life*. New York: Ballantine Books.

Atwater, P.M.H. and Morgan, D.H. (2005) *The Complete Idiot's Guide to Near Death Experiences*. Indianapolis: Alpha Books.

Bertherat, T. and Bernstein, C. (1976) *The Body Has Its Reasons*. New York: Avon Books.

Brunton, P. (1970) *A Search In Secret India*. New Delhi: B.I. Publications.

Cerminara, G. (1950) *Many Mansions*. New York: New American Library.

Dikshit, S.S. (ed.). (1973) *I Am That: Talks with Nisargadatta Maharaj*. Mumbai: Chetana (P) Ltd.

Dunn, J. (ed.). (1997) *Consciousness and the Absolute: The Final Talks with Nisargadatta Maharaj*. Mumbai: Chetana (P) Ltd.

Fiore, E. (1981) *You Have Been Here Before*. New York: Prentice Hall.

Gibran, K. (1998) *The Treasured Writings of Kahlil Gibran*. New York: Barnes and Noble Books.

Haber, H. (1963) *Stars, Men and Atoms*. New York: Golden Press.

Hardo, T. (2003) *Reincarnation*. New Delhi: Jaico Publications.

Hesse, H. (1993) *Siddhartha*. New Delhi: Rupa and Company.

Howarth, W. (ed.). (1981) *Walden and Other Writings by Henry David Thoreau*. New York: Modern Library.

Jerome, J.K. (1900) *Three Men in a Boat*. Bristol: JW Arrowsmith.

— — (1903) *Idle Thoughts of an Idle Fellow*. London: Hutchinson.

Khoo, T.K. (2014) "Universal Law of Reincarnation." Available at: http://www.kktanhp.com/reincarnation_htm.htm (Accessed: 18 August 2023).

Krishnamurti, J. (1927) *By What Authority*. Eerde, Holland: The Star Publishing Trust.

Kübler-Ross, E. (1969) *On Death and Dying*. New York: Macmillan.

— — (1975) *Death: The Final Stage of Growth*. New York: Simon & Schuster, Inc.

Langley, N. (1967) *Edgar Cayce on Reincarnation*. New York: Warner Books, Inc.

Lenz, Frederick. (1979) *Lifetimes*. New York: Fawcett Crest.

McWaters, B. (1983) *Conscious Evolution*. Wellingborough, UK: Turnstone Press.

Mitchell, S. (1943) *The Gospel According to Jesus*. New York: Harper Collins.

Moody, R.A., Jr. (1975) *Life After Life*. Atlanta: Mockingbird Books.

— — (1988) *The Light Beyond*. New York: Bantam Books.

Morse, M. (1992) *Transformed by the Light*. New York: Ballantine Books.

Perelman, Yakov. (1979) *Figures for Fun*. Moscow: Mir Publishers.

Petro, A. (2006) "Death Before Dying: A Love Experience." East Windsor Hill, CT, USA. Article in the newsletter *Vital Signs* of the International Association for Near-Death Studies, Vol. 25, No. 1. Available at: https://iands.org/research/publications/vital-signs/67-vs25no1petro.html?start=1 (Accessed: 18 August 2023).

Rajagopal, D. (ed.). (1991) *Commentaries on Living: Second Series*. Chennai: Krishnamurti Foundation of India.

Reeves, H. (1984) *Atoms of Silence*. Cambridge, MA, USA: The MIT Press.

Ritchie, Jean. (1996) *Death's Door*. New York: Dell Publishing.

Rogo, D.S. (1983) *Leaving the Body*. London: Prentice Hall International, Inc.

Sagan, C. et al. (2013) *Cosmos*. New York: Ballantine Books.

Sankaranarayanan, P. (1988) *What is Advaita?* Mumbai: Bharatiya Vidya Bhavan.

Singer, P. (1990) *Animal Liberation*. London: Pimlico Publication.

Solow, V. (1974) "I Died at 10:52 AM." Pleasantville, NY: Article in *Reader's Digest*, October 1974, pp. 178–182.

Suzuki, D.T. (1995) "The Meaning of Satori." Tiruvannamalai, Tamil Nadu, India: Article in *Mountain Path*, Jayanthi Issue, Ramanasramam, pp. 112–115.

Thorndike, E.L. and Barnhart, C.L. (1983) *Scott Foresman Intermediate Dictionary*. Illinois: Scott, Foresman and Company.

Timerman, J. (1981) *Prisoner without a name, Cell without a number*. New York: Alfred A. Knopf, Inc.

Tolle, E. (2001) *The Power of Now*. Mumbai: Yogi Impressions Books Pvt. Ltd.

— — (2003) *Stillness Speaks*. Mumbai: Yogi Impressions Books Pvt. Ltd.

Walsch, N.D. (1995) *Conversations with God: Book 1*. London: Hodder & Stoughton.

— — (2004) *Tomorrow's God*. New York: Atria Books.

Yale, J. (ed.). (1955) *What Vedanta Means to Me*. London: Rider & Company.

Glossary

Most of the non-English words given below are from Sanskrit.

Advaita – The state of oneness with everything in the universe, experienced under Satori and under the Universal Consciousness after Liberation.

Advaitic – Adjective of Advaita.

Ahankara – Egoism, Arrogance.

Artha – Wealth.

Athma – The Deeper Being in us. The True Self.

Athma Vichara – The path of inquiry towards the Athma.

Dharma – The quality of the practical life that is wholesome, holistic and righteous. Also, that which is always life-supportive and nondestructive.

Dharmic – The adjective of the noun Dharma.

Groupism – In the context of this book, it is used to represent the psychology of a group leading to herd mentality and fanaticism.

Guru – Teacher and a Guide, rolled into one!

Japam – Recitation of religious verses.

Jeevathma – The spark of the Divine in us; the essence that evolves through many lives to return to the source.

Kama – Enjoyment of pleasures.

Mantram – A Sanskrit spiritual or religious verse.

Moksha – Liberation.

Monism – The English term for the state of oneness experienced under Universal Consciousness.

Nadha – This Sanskrit word means sound. Nadha Yoga is the practice of listening to sounds.

Nirvana – The Buddhist term for Liberation.

Prakriti – The flow of nature with all its ingrained laws.

Sakshi Chaitanyam – Witness consciousness.

Sandhyakal – The meeting time of two different patterns, such as day and night.

Satori – It is a Japanese word – The experiencing of expansive Universal Consciousness when the mind is capable of receiving it.

The Primal Self – The Divine Spark in all of us; the Athma.

Veedu – It means a house or home in the Tamil language. In spirituality, it is used metaphorically to represent the Universal Consciousness to which we return on Liberation. It is like a homecoming.

Yogasana – A yoga posture.

MANTRA
BOOKS

EASTERN RELIGION & PHILOSOPHY
We publish books on Eastern religions and philosophies.
Books that aim to inform and explore the various traditions
that began in the East and have migrated West.
If you have enjoyed this book, why not tell other readers by
posting a review on your preferred book site.

Recent bestsellers from MANTRA BOOKS are:

The Way Things Are
A Living Approach to Buddhism
Lama Ole Nydahl
An introduction to the teachings of the Buddha, and how to
make use of these teachings in everyday life.
Paperback: 978-1-84694-042-2 ebook: 978-1-78099-845-9

Back to the Truth
5000 Years of Advaita
Dennis Waite
A demystifying guide to Advaita for both those new to, and those
familiar with this ancient, non-dualist philosophy from India.
Paperback: 978-1-90504-761-1 ebook: 978-184694-624-0

Shinto: A celebration of Life
Aidan Rankin
Introducing a gentle but powerful spiritual pathway reconnecting
humanity with Great Nature and affirming all aspects of life.
Paperback: 978-1-84694-438-3 ebook: 978-1-84694-738-4

In the Light of Meditation
Mike George
A comprehensive introduction to the practice of meditation
and the spiritual principles behind it. A 10 lesson meditation
programme with CD and internet support.
Paperback: 978-1-90381-661-5

A Path of Joy
Popping into Freedom
Paramananda Ishaya
A simple and joyful path to spiritual enlightenment.
Paperback: 978-1-78279-323-6 ebook: 978-1-78279-322-9

The Less Dust the More Trust
Participating in The Shamatha Project, Meditation and
Science
Adeline van Waning, MD PhD
The inside-story of a woman participating in frontline
meditation research, exploring the interfaces of mind-practice,
science and psychology.
Paperback: 978-1-78099-948-7 ebook: 978-1-78279-657-2

I Know How To Live, I Know How To Die
The Teachings of Dadi Janki: A warm, radical, and life-
affirming view of who we are, where we come from,
and what time is calling us to do
Neville Hodgkinson
Life and death are explored in the context of frontier science
and deep soul awareness.
Paperback: 978-1-78535-013-9 ebook: 978-1-78535-014-6

Living Jainism
An Ethical Science
Aidan Rankin, Kanti V. Mardia
A radical new perspective on science rooted in intuitive
awareness and deductive reasoning.
Paperback: 978-1-78099-912-8 ebook: 978-1-78099-911-1

Ordinary Women, Extraordinary Wisdom
The Feminine Face of Awakening
Rita Marie Robinson
A collection of intimate conversations with female spiritual
teachers who live like ordinary women, but are engaged
with their true natures.
Paperback: 978-1-84694-068-2 ebook: 978-1-78099-908-1

The Way of Nothing
Nothing in the Way
Paramananda Ishaya
A fresh and lighthearted exploration of the
amazing reality of nothingness.
Paperback: 978-1-78279-307-6 ebook: 978-1-78099-840-4

Readers of ebooks can buy or view any of these bestsellers by
clicking on the live link in the title. Most titles are published
in paperback and as an ebook. Paperbacks are available in
traditional bookshops. Both print and ebook formats are
available online.

Find more titles and sign up to our readers' newsletter at
www.collectiveinkbooks.com/mind-body-spirit. Follow
us on Facebook at facebook.com/OBook and
Twitter at twitter.com/obooks